THE PROPHECY OF
HOSEA

THE PROPHECY OF HOSEA

"I will love them freely"

Cyril Tennant

THE CHRISTADELPHIAN
404 SHAFTMOOR LANE
BIRMINGHAM B28 8SZ

1987

First published 1987

ISBN 0 85189 120 9

Printed and bound in Great Britain
by Billing & Sons Limited, Worcester.

CONTENTS

ACKNOWLEDGEMENTS

THE writer wishes to acknowledge the help received in the clarification of some of the more obscure verses from *The Minor Prophets* by E. B. Pusey and a commentary on Hosea by E. C. Woollcombe.

It is almost superfluous to acknowledge our indebtedness to Robert Young for his *Analytical Concordance* but it must be said that no single work has contributed more to the opening up of sound principles of Bible study for every student.

A book which was not consulted during this study but which was read some thirty years ago and which has left a lasting impression is *The Heart and Holiness of God* by G. Campbell Morgan. It may even be that some of Morgan's phrases have remained with me and have crept into the text without my being conscious of it. Should this be so, it is an additional tribute to his treatment of his subject.

Cover Picture

Thanks are expressed to Cyril Cooper for the loan of a colour transparency depicting flowers in the land of Israel.

INTRODUCTION

THE prophecy of Hosea is unique for its sympathetic and moving treatment of God "receiving graciously" those who render to Him "the calves of their lips". There is a depth of feeling which is born of Hosea's personal grief in his relationship with an adulterous wife. Under God's direction, his handling of this domestic tragedy fits him to be God's mouthpiece to Israel and through her to all who will listen.

Although Hosea's own story is not the theme of the book, it is nevertheless always to be seen just below the surface. Because of it, Hosea is able to enter into the spirit of God's message to Israel as He rebukes, pleads with and ultimately gives His own Son to die for those who will listen.

The message is stern and shows that there can be no compromise with sin! It shows the nature of sin to be such that nothing but the unqualified love of God could even begin to conceive a plan of salvation, and it reveals in real terms the cost at which that salvation was to be purchased.

The prophecy is also unique in another way. Just as Jesus was the teacher who excelled in the use of parables, even though such had been used by many before his day, so Hosea excels in the use of Biblical names. They become alive in his hands and add depth to his message. So it is essential that we spend time examining the names he uses, both for their meanings and also the circumstances in which they occur in the Scriptures.

Hosea's message is in the first instance for the rebel ten-tribe kingdom of Israel and it is illustrated by the real life parable of Hosea and Gomer. It is, however, a message which makes abundantly clear that God's purpose will only be accomplished in a remnant which will be taken from amongst all the twelve tribes and also from amongst the Gentiles. This means that the message is for us. It is about our salvation. To use Hosea's own words, "There God spake with us".

THE TIMES OF HOSEA
(HOSEA 1:1)

Year B.C.	Kings of Israel	Kings of Judah	Reign	Notes
785	Jeroboam II		41 yrs	
790		Uzziah	52 yrs	Also called Azariah
744	Zachariah		6 mths	Murdered by Shallum
744	*Shallum		1 mth	Murdered by Menahem
744	*Menahem		10 yrs	
737	Pekahiah		2 yrs	Murdered by Pekah
736	*Pekah		20 yrs	Murdered by Hoshea
758		Jotham	16 yrs	
742		Ahaz	16 yrs	
729	*Hoshea		9 yrs	ASSYRIAN CAPTIVITY
726		Hezekiah	29 yrs	

Notes

1. There appears to have been some overlapping in some of the reigns, and historians differ on the above dates.
2. The time is measured off by use of the kings of Judah, Jeroboam II only being mentioned to commence the period.
3. * Indicates the beginning of a new dynasty. It will be seen how violent the kingdom of Israel was in that there were eight dynasties from its formation and five of those were during Hosea's ministry!

1

THE BRIDEGROOM AND HIS BRIDE

VERSES 1-3

*T*HE word of the LORD that came unto Hosea, the
son of Beeri, in the days of Uzziah, Jotham, Ahaz,
and Hezekiah, kings of Judah, and in the days of
Jeroboam the son of Joash, king of Israel.
2 The beginning of the word of the LORD by Hosea.
And the LORD said to Hosea, Go, take unto thee a wife
of whoredoms and children of whoredoms: for the land
hath committed great whoredom, departing from the
LORD.
3 So he went and took Gomer the daughter of Diblaim;
which conceived, and bare him a son.

HOSEA was selected by God to be the main actor in a real life
drama which would prepare him for the special task God had
in store for him. He was to be the bearer of God's message, but not
before he had experienced its detail in his own life. In a much less,
but still demanding way he, like Jesus, was to be personally
involved in the salvation which he must preach. He is introduced
to us by his name which means *Jah is help* and is a type of
Immanuel, God with us, the one through whom God would effect
His plan of redemption, a plan which though including Israel would
be for the whole of mankind.

Thus the tone and pattern of the book are set. It is about God's
personal involvement in man's salvation. In the first instance it is
directly concerned with the ten tribes of Israel which under the
leadership of Jeroboam had broken away from Judah. But, as we

1

shall see, there is also a message for Judah and indeed for all who will listen, whether Jew or Gentile. The climax of the message is in the formation of a new Bride through the redeeming work of Jesus, only made possible because our God is a merciful God.

Jesus claimed nothing for himself; his words and his works were, he said, of his Father, and throughout his life he drank deeply of "the fountain of living waters" (a description which God uses of Himself, Jeremiah 2:13; 17:13) and we are not surprised to find this typified in Hosea, whose father's name was Beeri, meaning *my well* or *welling forth*. Nor are we surprised to read of the promise to the faithful: "With joy shall ye draw water out of the wells of salvation" (Isaiah 12:3). All is of God; there is no other source of strength, and all who fail to recognise this will perish in their weakness.

This message is also hidden in the names of Jeroboam, *enlarger*, and those of the kings of Judah whose names are listed in the first verse—Uzziah: *Jah is strong*; Jotham: *Jah is perfect*; Ahaz: *He holds* and Hezekiah: *Jah is strength*, kings from whom the ten tribes were now separated. Under the delusion of making themselves great, they had in rebellion broken away from the only real source of strength and perfection; therefore as a kingdom they would perish. Judah would survive the captivity, but not the kingdom of Israel. It would be a mere remnant which would be delivered only by seeking one king with Judah. All this is summarised by God in the words recorded in 13:9: "O Israel, thou hast destroyed thyself; but in me is thine help." The world boasts of many "lovers", attractions in so many different guises, lovers by whom "many strong men have been slain" (Proverbs 7:26). Unless this displacement of affection is recognised for what is is, man must perish under its influence.

The human mind finds it difficult to understand how God can desire to save man who is so unlovely and unlovable; how, whilst man persists in walking his own way, God can at the same time be planning a scheme for his redemption. Yet this is the basic truth, so clearly and helpfully revealed through Hosea and finally achieved "in that whilst we were yet sinners, Christ died for us". Hosea will also teach us of God's judgement, how those things which so often appear to men to be pure acts of punishment are in fact remedial—they are, as we read in the margin for 2:14, God's way of "speaking to her heart".

Having selected Hosea, type of the Bridegroom, it is now necessary that he shall have a bride. In the first instance she will represent the ten tribes of Israel, but in the fuller sense she will represent the Bride of Christ—but let us permit Hosea to tell his own story.

Gomer is chosen. Her name, meaning *complete* or *perfect*, suggests that she had not been guilty of adulterous behaviour before her marriage. This conforms to the teaching of Jeremiah 2:21: "Yet had I planted thee a noble vine, wholly a right seed: how then art thou turned into the degenerate plant of a strange vine unto me?" It also completes the parallel of verse 2: "For the land hath committed great whoredom, departing from the LORD" and is supported by the fact that only the last two of Gomer's children were spoken of as children of whoredom, since chapter 2 contains words which were to be spoken by the first child about the others.

However, although the above may be true, God who commanded Hosea to take a wife, knew from the beginning what kind of person she was and would later prove herself to be: hence His description of her. Just as Cain was a murderer from the beginning and confirmed the fact by murdering Abel, so Gomer, though technically "perfect", was an adulteress from the beginning. The seeds of wickedness were already there. In common with the whole of mankind, her heart was "deceitful above all things, and desperately wicked". This desperate plight of man is made so much the worse by his deceitfulness which prevents him from recognising it! Therefore if he is to be saved, the first move must come from God, and how thankful we should be that He has taken the initiative.

To complete the picture, Gomer is seen to be the daughter of Diblaim, whose name means *a double cluster of figs*. Like Israel whom she represents, she is a child of pleasure or fruitfulness and does not appreciate the source of her blessings which she squanders upon her lovers (2:8,9). It is more than a coincidence that Gomer is the daughter of one whose name means *a double cluster of figs;* and the ten tribes whom she represents are given the poetic name of Ephraim throughout this prophecy, which means *double fruitfulness.* Additionally, Israel's downfall was hastened by Jeroboam, whose name as we have already noted means *enlarger.*

The principle of "waxing fat and kicking" is a constant theme of warning in the pages of Scripture, but so deceitful is the heart of man that whilst he is able to see the danger for others he may miss it completely for himself. He is always different. He can always cope. After all someone must make the money for the family and for ecclesial needs. He will covet the wealth of Abraham but will fail to follow Abraham's example and wait for God to bless as and when He shall see fit.

So the stage is set for the real life drama. Hosea has been chosen as the vessel through whom, by word and experience, God will reveal the deep and moving things connected with His plan of salvation. Gomer has also been chosen that she through her self-generated misery and despair might represent, firstly the ten tribes in their fruitless rebellion and that to which it led, but more fully—every man's need of a Saviour!

CHILDREN OF WHOREDOMS

VERSES 3-11

3 So he went and took Gomer the daughter of Diblaim; which conceived, and bare him a son.

4 And the LORD said unto him, Call his name Jezreel; for yet a little while, and I will avenge the blood of Jezreel upon the house of Jehu, and will cause to cease the kingdom of the house of Israel.

5 And it shall come to pass at that day, that I will break the bow of Israel in the valley of Jezreel.

6 And she conceived again, and bare a daughter. And God said unto him, Call her name Lo-ruhamah:

4

*for I will no more have mercy upon the house of Israel;
but I will utterly take them away.*

*7 But I will have mercy upon the house of Judah, and
will save them by the LORD their God, and will not save
them by bow, nor by sword, nor by battle, by horses,
nor by horsemen.*

*8 Now when she had weaned Lo-ruhamah, she con-
ceived, and bare a son.*

*9 Then said God, Call his name Lo-ammi: for ye are
not my people, and I will not be your God.*

*10 Yet the number of the children of Israel shall be as
the sand of the sea, which cannot be measured nor
numbered; and it shall come to pass, that in the place
where it was said unto them, Ye are not my people, there
it shall be said unto them, Ye are the sons of the living
God.*

*11 Then shall the children of Judah and the children of
Israel be gathered together, and appoint themselves one
head, and they shall come up out of the land: for great
shall be the day of Jezreel.*

Gomer's three children are, under God's instruction, given names
which describe the fruits of Israel's wickedness and the utter isolation into which it has led her. The first child was born to Hosea
(1:3) and represents true Israel, the faithful of God whose duty it
is to speak forth God's message to "an evil and adulterous generation" (2:1). After his birth, Gomer is "tempted ... drawn away
of her own lust, and enticed ... bringeth forth sin" (James
1:14,15)—she gives birth to two children in quick succession (1:8),
but they are the children of whoredom (2:4).

Gomer has a great capacity for sin and is unable to contain her
zeal to bring forth the children of unrighteousness. Not only is she
twice as ready to bear the children of sin as she is to bear the child
of wedlock, but in so doing is prepared to see the destruction of her
marriage (2:1,2). She is a perfect type of fallen humanity who will

5

spare no effort to serve ambition, greed and lust but who is slow to serve God.

Jezreel, the first-born, who is to be the faithful witness, carries in his name the message *God sows*, a message which has three parts—the first to the house of Jehu (v. 4), the second to the house of Israel (v. 4) and the third to the "sons of the living God" (v. 10). All three parts were prophetic and the first two, having already come to pass, provide the basis for confidence that the third will also be fulfilled.

Jehu had been instrumental in ensuring that Ahab reaped that which he had sown, and for his labours was promised that his children, to the fourth generation, would sit upon the throne of Israel. Nevertheless, because he had not departed from the sins of Jeroboam, he was told that his house would cease (2 Kings 10:30,31). This prophecy was fulfilled when Zachariah was slain (2 Kings 15:8-10) and thus was avenged "the blood of Jezreel upon the house of Jehu".

The kingdom of Israel (the ten tribes) continued under different dynasties until the reign of Hoshea, who was dethroned by the king of Assyria. He also carried the ten tribes into captivity, thus causing the kingdom of the house of Israel to cease (2 Kings 17:6; Hosea 1:4; 10:15). Hosea makes it abundantly clear both here and elsewhere that the ten tribes will never again appear as a kingdom. Their future can only be sought along with that of the two tribes, in the one king who shall come to reign at God's command (1:11).

We shall return to the third aspect of "God's sowing" when we consider Hosea chapter 2. But before doing so we must look at the names of the two children of whoredom.

There is a dreadful finality in the cutting off of the ten tribes. The house of Israel was to cease! They were to be utterly taken away. They were to be no more. This dissolution of the rebellious tribes is foretold in the meanings of the names of the "children of whoredom", the first of which is Lo-ruhamah, *not pitied* or *not having obtained mercy*, and the second, Lo-ammi, *not my people*. Israel had come to the end of the line. Judah would survive by

6

God's strength (1:7), but the ten tribes would never again exist as a separate kingdom. There could be no further extension of mercy. Having by their behaviour declared themselves to be "not God's people", He would no longer be their God. As the children of whoredom were not Hosea's, so Israel were not now God's people. To borrow a figure from the apostle Paul, Israel had become "joined to an harlot" (1 Corinthians 6:16); the separation was Israel's doing but it was now final.

It is part of the wonder of God's salvation, that anything could be rescued out of the desperate plight into which Israel had fallen. What possible hope could there be for any of their descendants? Hosea explains to us how this situation, which is really only typical of that of the whole of mankind, is in fact resolved by God without there being any compromise with sin.

There is more than a hint of this solution to be found in the last two verses of this chapter which, when taken together with the apostle Paul's exposition of them (Romans 9:24-33), reveal that there will be a remnant from both Judah and Israel joined together with believing Gentiles to be called "the sons of the living God". They are the redeemed out of all nations, reached by God's saving arm and born again by the power of His word so as gladly to accept the rule of the Lord's anointed.

Perhaps it will not be out of place at this point to comment on the structure of the book of Hosea and draw attention to God's method of teaching by a process of gentle repetition, a method which firmly establishes the fundamentals of God's salvation by keeping them continually before us.

Firstly the whole story is drawn in broad outline. There then follows a series of studies, each of which returns to a different point in the narrative to add extra detail before taking a slightly different route to the climax. The process could be illustrated diagramatically by a series of arches, the first of which would span the whole story whilst each of the others, though starting at a different point within the first arch would finish at the same point. In this way we are continually reminded of the essentials of our salvation whilst further light is being shed upon them. In addition we are encouraged by the oft repeated glimpses of the Kingdom.

The gentle repetition of the various principles ensures that detail is added in a way in which they can be readily absorbed and in a context which illustrates them. The reader is carried along, never being taken out of his depth but always learning something new. This is one of the main reasons why the books of the Bible seldom contain their messages in chronological order and why it is so damaging to the message to try to rearrange the contents so that they become chronological. This is God's method and it is folly to tamper with it!

2

AMMI AND RUHAMAH

VERSE 1

*S*AY *ye unto your brethren, Ammi; and to your sisters, Ruhamah.*

ORIGINALLY there were no breaks between the chapters, the chapter and verse arrangement being adopted for ease of reference; and whilst all agree that such an arrangement is indispensable for the student, it must also be stated that the arrangement does sometimes affect the sense of the text. This is the case here, since the first verse of this chapter is really part of the climax which is reached in the previous chapter.

The kingdom of God has been established. A people has been introduced and described as "the sons of the living God", which includes descendants of Israel and Judah. All this is illustrated by a play on the meanings of the names of the children of whoredom, Lo-ammi and Lo-ruhamah, which continues in such a way that their meanings are completely changed. The teaching of verse 1 becomes, Say unto those who were not my people (Lo-ammi), "Ammi" (*my people*); and to those not having obtained mercy (Lo-ruhamah), "Ruhamah" (*having obtained mercy*). The condition of each child is completely reversed.

We might well wonder how this could be. How, after the forthright condemnation of the previous verses, could the people possibly be accepted in this way? Although we have already seen the answer hinted at in the reference made to this quotation by the apostle Paul (Romans 9:22-26), Hosea has not as yet revealed the secret. Indeed, in the section we are considering, he still only

9

begins to explain it. His real purpose in this section is to re-introduce the plight of the ten tribes and in accordance with God's method of teaching, add further details which spell out more clearly the utter hopelessness of their case. Then, in broad outline only, he speaks of God's salvation as he reaches out to the grand climax of His purpose. It is left to a later section to return to this point and supply the missing details.

"SHE IS NOT MY WIFE; I AM NOT HER HUSBAND"
VERSES 2-4

2 Plead with your mother, plead: for she is not my wife, neither am I her husband: let her therefore put away her whoredoms out of her sight, and her adulteries from between her breasts;

3 Lest I strip her naked, and set her as in the day that she was born, and make her as a wilderness, and set her like a dry land, and slay her with thirst.

4 And I will not have mercy upon her children; for they be the children of whoredoms.

Jezreel is sent to plead with his mother who is living in blissful ignorance of her true condition. "For she did not know . . . " (v. 8), and in this ignorance she is representative of Israel whose lack of knowledge becomes a point for special exhortation (4:1-6).

The awful truth which she must now face is, "She is not my wife, neither am I her husband". This is an expansion of Hosea's teaching concerning Lo-ruhamah and Lo-ammi, and is designed to drive home to Israel the utter desolation which she has chosen. The basis of the appeal is the broken marriage of Gomer with Hosea, and three important principles emerge which may be noted at this point:

1. the serious consequences of adulterous behaviour upon the marriage bond;

2. by parallel, the serious nature of the sin of spiritual adultery, and

3. the wonder that God is still ready and willing to save.

10

Marriage is intended to be a lifelong relationship; of that there can be no doubt, as reference to the following passages will show: Genesis 2:24; Matthew 19:5; Romans 7:2; 1 Corinthians 7:10,11 and Malachi 2:16. To break such a relationship is to incur God's hatred and as such is a very serious thing; the gravity of Israel's sin is underlined, being described by Gomer's adulterous behaviour. Her adultery had broken her marriage: "She is not my wife . . . I will not have mercy upon her children . . . for their mother hath played the harlot . . . " (2:2,4,5).

Under the Law of Moses this truth was enforced in that the offending person was stoned to death; thus the gravity of the sin was seen and its effect upon the marriage made known to all. Under the Christian dispensation the apostle Paul explains that adulterous behaviour has the effect of taking the guilty person from his professed marriage, and joining him to an harlot (1 Corinthians 6:15,16). The adulterous act is a violation of the intimacy of the marriage relationship.

That which is true in the natural marriage relationship is seen to be true in the husband/wife relationship of God with Israel. Here in Hosea 2:2, and in several other verses spread throughout the prophets, God is seen to view the marriage as broken. It must be noted in those verses which speak of God as giving a bill of divorcement, that He is only confirming what has already taken place because of the adulterous conduct of Israel. Their prolonged adultery had demonstrated their flagrant disregard of the holy marriage contract. Each of the following verses should be read in its context to obtain the full import of the teaching:

Jeremiah 31:32 " . . . which my covenant they brake, although I was an husband unto them."

Ezekiel 16:38 "And I will judge thee, as women that break wedlock . . . are judged."

Jeremiah 3:8 " . . . Israel (had) committed adultery I had put her away, and given her a bill of divorce."

Such then was the desperate situation of Gomer and, more important to our consideration, of Israel whom she represented.

Gomer was entitled to no legal rights with Hosea, just as Israel, having broken her covenant with God, could no longer claim His blessings.

So blinded is Gomer by her sin, that she assumes the things which she has received have come from her lovers with whom she squanders them and Hosea develops this real life parable to show how Israel, not knowing that her blessings came from God, used them in the worship of Baal (2:8). This particular twist of mind is not to be found only with Israel. The lesson that man does not live by bread alone but by every word which proceeds from the mouth of God, is one which all need to learn and remember—especially when times may be hard.

THREE STAGES OF RECONCILIATION
VERSES 5-23

5 For their mother hath played the harlot: she that conceived them hath done shamefully: for she said, I will go after my lovers, that give me my bread and my water, my wool and my flax, mine oil and my drink.

6 Therefore, behold, I will hedge up thy way with thorns, and make a wall, that she shall not find her paths.

7 And she shall follow after her lovers, but she shall not overtake them; and she shall seek them, but shall not find them: then shall she say, I will go and return to my first husband; for then was it better with me than now.

8 For she did not know that I gave her corn, and wine, and oil, and multiplied her silver and gold, which they prepared for Baal.

9 Therefore will I return, and take away my corn in the time thereof, and my wine in the season thereof, and will recover my wool and my flax given to cover her nakedness.

10 And now will I discover her lewdness in the sight of her lovers, and none shall deliver her out of mine hand.

11 I will also cause all her mirth to cease, her feast days, her new moons, and her sabbaths, and all her solemn feasts.

12 And I will destroy her vines and her fig trees, whereof she hath said, These are my rewards that my lovers have given me: and I will make them a forest, and the beasts of the field shall eat them.

13 And I will visit upon her the days of Baalim, wherein she burned incense to them, and she decked herself with her earrings and her jewels, and she went after her lovers, and forgat me, saith the LORD.

14 Therefore, behold, I will allure her, and bring her into the wilderness, and speak comfortably unto her.

15 And I will give her her vineyards from thence, and the valley of Achor for a door of hope: and she shall sing there, as in the days of her youth, and as in the day when she came up out of the land of Egypt.

16 And it shall be at that day, saith the LORD, that thou shalt call me Ishi; and shalt call me no more Baali.

17 For I will take away the names of Baalim out of her mouth, and they shall no more be remembered by their name.

18 And in that day will I make a covenant for them with the beasts of the field, and with the fowls of heaven, and with the creeping things of the ground: and I will break the bow and the sword and the battle out of the earth, and will make them to lie down safely.

19 And I will betroth thee unto me for ever; yea, I will betroth thee unto me in righteousness, and in judgment, and in lovingkindness, and in mercies.

20 I will even betroth thee unto me in faithfulness: and thou shalt know the LORD.

21 And it shall come to pass in that day, I will hear, saith the LORD, I will hear the heavens, and they shall hear the earth;

22 And the earth shall hear the corn, and the wine, and the oil; and they shall hear Jezreel.

23 And I will sow her unto me in the earth; and I will have mercy upon her that had not obtained mercy; and I will say to them which were not my people, Thou art my people; and they shall say, Thou art my God.

The hint that reconciliation was possible is seen in verse 2: "Let her therefore put away her whoredoms . . . lest I . . . ", and as we pass down the chapter we quickly realise that what may at first appear to be retributive judgement, is in fact God's remedial action. Note carefully the steps which could lead Israel to redemption and which illustrate principles in God's handling of all His children who transgress. There are three steps, each commencing with the word "therefore" and which together reach out far beyond Israel's current experience to a fulfilment in God's kingdom with a people perfected by His love.

The first step is to block Gomer's way to her lovers (Israel's way to idolatry) in the hope that being unable to find them, she will return to Hosea (Israel to God). "Therefore, behold, I will hedge up thy way with thorns, and make a wall, that she shall not find her paths. And she shall follow after her lovers, but she shall not overtake them; . . . then shall she say, I will go and return to my first husband; for then was it better with me than now" (vv. 6,7). God would actually make it more difficult for Israel to commit idolatry than to serve Him. He will in fact cause the sinner to be afflicted in his godless pursuits, that their futility might be recognised before it is too late. Jesus reminds us of this principle when he lists persecution as an added blessing (Mark 10:30).

In actual practice, God humbled Israel by famine and pestilence that she might learn (Deuteronomy 8:3), but the lessons were not heeded. Instead, so intent were they upon their course of wickedness that they dragged themselves through the hedge of thorns to reach their idols. Humiliated, scathed and distressed, heedless of the hand of God which would prevent them, they pressed forwards towards their wicked objectives. It is a very strange thing that whilst imaginary obstacles will very often deter a man from true worship, nothing will hinder him in the gratification of his worldly ambitions. He will even sacrifice his health, family and ultimately his eternal well-being for that which "endureth but for a season". It was as though God must gather together all the sins of the world and place them upon His own Son before man would begin to recognise his need for salvation. The hedge of thorns must first become a crown to be pressed down upon the head of the one who would be "made sin for us", before even a small remnant would mourn in contemplation of his wounds and in admission that their sins had been the cause.

In anticipation of Israel's failure to heed the first warning, God had already prepared a second one. Since they will still seek their "lovers" even though the way has been made difficult, God would now take away His blessings to reveal that they had in fact come from Him and not, as they supposed, from their lovers: "Therefore will I return, and take away my corn in the time thereof, and my wine in the season thereof, and will recover my wool and my flax given to cover her nakedness." The blessings of corn, wine, oil, silver, gold, wool and flax, seven in number representing the perfection of God's gifts, would go. But worse still, God would also take away her spiritual blessings. Her solemn feasts and sabbaths would also cease.

This was a further remedial act designed to bring Israel back to her God. How could she exist without the necessities of life? Something of her impending poverty is foreshadowed in Gomer's helplessness when she was forsaken by her lovers. She would surely have perished, had not Hosea intervened at God's command.

This second stage is really a softening process leading up to

God's final appeal, but it is a very strong reminder to us of the words of Jesus: "Seek ye first the kingdom of God and his righteousness and all these things will be added unto you." To seek God and His kingdom first of all, is to embark upon a way of life which is richly blessed by much more than the mere necessities of life; whilst to seek first the things of this life will inevitably result in the loss of all.

Steps one and two, though each is remedial and complete for those who will listen, together become preparatory for the third. With the way to her false gods made difficult, and with the source of her supplies cut off, it was hoped that Israel would now be prepared to listen to God as He spoke "to her heart". "Therefore I will allure her, and bring her into the wilderness, and speak to her heart (R.V. margin). And I will give her her vineyards from thence, and the valley of Achor for a door of hope . . ." In the wilderness of her experience, God would yet plead with Israel, and slowly, as she was able to receive them, He would once more satisfy her needs. This chapter is prophetic. Israel did not respond and repent, therefore the kingdom of the ten tribes ceased to exist. It is a remnant taken from a future generation which will in penitence receive the blessings which are spoken of.

Although we are not specifically told so in this chapter, we know from elsewhere in the book of Hosea and also from the comments made by the apostle Paul upon the expression "them which were not a people", that the remnant will also include some from amongst the kingdom of Judah and some from amongst the Gentiles. The picture once more is of the redeemed from all nations. It is a new bride with a new covenant (v. 18), this time betrothed to Him for ever (v. 19). This is an everlasting betrothal, formed in "righteousness" and in "judgement" and in "faithfulness" (vv. 19,20). In that day, that redeemed remnant will call God, "Ishi" (my husband) and not "Baali" (my lord or master).

This bride will be brought forth out of great tribulation as described in the book of Revelation, for we are told in the 15th verse of this chapter that the valley of Achor will be a door of hope.

16

"Achor" means *troubling*, a fact which is amply demonstrated in Joshua 7. It is paradoxical that "troubling" should become an entrance to hope! But tribulation *is* remedial. It is preparatory to God speaking to our hearts. If we will but listen, tribulation will become a door of hope to us. Surely as the Psalmist writes: "The Lord is nigh unto them that are of a broken heart", but he only saveth "such as be of a contrite spirit" (Psalm 34:18).

This great day which witnesses the birth of a new bride also sees the forming of a new earth, a changed earth, an earth with its curse removed. Verses 21 and 22 describe a sequence of events which lead to this new and fruitful age, events which commence with God's sowing (Jezreel). Note the sequence: "I will hear the heavens, and they shall hear the earth; and the earth shall hear the corn, and the wine, and the oil; and they shall hear Jezreel." The day of Jezreel, of God's sowing, of tribulation which opens into a door of hope for the faithful, sees also a responsive and fruitful earth. This same day is described by the apostle Paul in Romans 8:19-22 where, with the substitution in the Revised Version of the word *creation* for the word *creature*, the sense is made even more clear:

"For the earnest expectation of the *creation* waiteth for the manifestation of the sons of God. For the *creation* was made subject to vanity, not willingly, but by reason of him who hath subjected the same in hope, because the *creation* itself also shall be delivered from the bondage of corruption into the glorious liberty of the children of God. For we know that the whole *creation* groaneth and travaileth in pain together until now."

It is a picture in which the apostle shows the redeemed emerging from suffering into a world freed from the curse made necessary by Adam's transgression and finally enveloped in the love of God. It is this day which Hosea also saw, and which he so clearly showed to be the work of God.

The last verse of this chapter uses the various names of all three children in a description of the duties of the redeemed in the

17

Millennial age. The new bride is *sown* in the earth, not *scattered* as the old bride had been, but sown to produce the fruit of righteousness in that age. Sent out amongst those of the mortal population who have survived the most dreadful shaking that this world will ever have known, the new bride is to teach the principles of God's salvation of which she will then be a part.

3

"GO YET, LOVE A WOMAN. . ."
VERSES 1-2

*T*HEN *said the* LORD *unto me, Go yet, love a woman beloved of her friend, yet an adulteress, according to the love of the* LORD *toward the children of Israel, who look to other gods, and love flagons of wine.*

2 So I bought her to me for fifteen pieces of silver, and for an homer of barley, and an half homer of barley:

*S*OUND Bible exposition is based upon two very simple but often ignored steps. They are:
1. What is the Bible actually saying? and
2. What does the Bible mean by what it is saying?

So often the meaning is sought from a superficial reading of the text with the context being almost completely ignored. This leads to fanciful interpretations of Scripture and even to stretching the meanings of words to make them fit in with a previously conceived theory. Before attempting an explanation one must be sure that everything possible has been done to ensure a correct understanding of what is actually written. This is the only way to listen to what God is saying and failure to achieve this will not only cause one to miss the truth, it may also lead to sin through teaching others that which is not Bible teaching.

Turning to the third chapter of Hosea's prophecy, we must then ask ourselves, "What is God asking of Hosea?" Is He commanding Hosea to take another wife, a wife who is an adulteress? A superficial reading of verse 1 might lead us to this unsavoury conclusion, but a careful reading will show that this cannot be so. That which is being commanded is in accordance "with God's love towards the children of Israel". The people who had been cut off because of their transgressions are yet to be loved by God and their future is to be illustrated in Hosea's own relationship with Gomer. Clearly then, Hosea is being told that his dealings with Gomer are not yet complete. He must find her and love her as God loves wayward Israel. Painful though this may be to him, he must do it, and much of what God knew he had already suffered and was still to endure is reflected in the words "Go yet".

The prophet Isaiah also describes this stage in God's salvation in words which are very similar to those of Hosea: "For the LORD hath called thee as a woman forsaken and grieved in spirit, and a wife of youth, when thou wast refused, saith thy God. For a small moment have I forsaken thee; but with great mercies will I gather thee" (Isaiah 54:6,7). We have already been caused to wonder how a people so utterly and completely cut off could ever have a future with God—Hosea is now to explain how this is possible.

It will be noted that Hosea was only given one command: "Go love a woman." All that follows is as a result of that love! This is typical of man's salvation which was not sought, which was undeserved and which is the product of God's love.

The Gomer whom Hosea now sought, was much changed. Sin had done its worst. Something of her utter degradation is to be seen in the fact that Hosea could purchase her and in the price which he paid for her—fifteen pieces of silver and a homer and a half of barley. The total cash value a mere 37.5 shekels, just a little more than the price which was paid for a slave in those days! This was not the Gomer who had attracted to herself many lovers. She was now unwanted and available for a paltry price. Now she would know from whom her blessings had previously come! Now that it was almost too late she would know the cost of her folly. The fact that it was not too late was a reflection of God's great compassion towards the sinner and His desire that all shall come to repentance.

We may wonder what Hosea's thoughts were when he first saw this much changed woman and what there was in her to commend her to his love. Not only had she left him as she went in search of her many lovers but she was now only a shadow of her former self. She had paid the price of her sin. How could Hosea carry out God's command to love her? To seek her out, yes, but to love her as he had done before, would that not be asking too much?

The answer is to be found in the words "according to the love of the LORD . . .". This was a divinely controlled, real life parable; Hosea's love was to be in accordance with God's love for Israel.

There can be no comparison between that which passes for human love and that which is exhibited by God. Human love always requires some object beyond itself to excite it, whereas God loves because He is love! Human love is self-rewarding, since it is fed by its own experiences, whereas God's love flows from Him for the benefit of the one loved by Him. Though on occasions human love may appear to be selfless it is nevertheless an emotion which is generated by what is seen or felt; there is always some external cause to which that love is a response. By contrast God's love is truly selfless in that He has shown it towards man who is totally undeserving, unlovely and unlovable.

It was therefore in demonstration of the love of God towards Israel that Hosea now sought Gomer and even though there would be little to commend her to him, having found her, he must free her from her slavery; hence we read, "So I bought her". It was in the outworking of this God-given love, that Hosea explained how it was possible for God to reach those who through wilful perversity were estranged from Him. A price had to be paid that the slave might go free. But it was not with the paltry price paid for a slave that God purchased man's redemption; it was with the precious blood of His own Son: "Herein is love, not that we loved God, but that he loved us, and sent his Son to be the propitiation for our sins" (1 John 4:10).

21

"THOU SHALT ABIDE FOR ME MANY DAYS"
Verses 3-5

3 And I said unto her, Thou shalt abide for me many days; thou shalt not play the harlot, and thou shalt not be for another man: so will I also be for thee.

4 For the children of Israel shall abide many days without a king, and without a prince, and without a sacrifice, and without an image, and without an ephod, and without teraphim:

5 Afterward shall the children of Israel return, and seek the LORD their God, and David their king; and shall fear the LORD and his goodness in the latter days.

Let us not assume that salvation is an automatic thing dependent only upon the love of God. It is abundantly true that the first step had to be taken by God, that before man was even conscious of his need God should set in motion the machinery for his redemption, that whilst "we were yet sinners" Christ should die for us. But before the salvation for which Jesus died can be ours we must become personally involved. This facet of our salvation is explained by Hosea in the remaining verses of this chapter.

Although Gomer's freedom had been purchased, she was not given full marital status immediately. We read: "Thou shalt abide for me many days; thou shalt not play the harlot, and thou shalt not be for another man." Over a period of time Gomer must prove her penitence; there must be no returning to her lovers, and in "abiding" for Hosea she must prove her changed mind. She would be with Hosea but not yet fully as his wife. In all this she would demonstrate how God would deal with Israel.

However, before we turn to consider Israel we must pause to notice in this pattern an example of the required chastity of those who would be the bride of Christ. The days following baptism must demonstrate the vows made; our behaviour must speak of our yearning for the return of the one who has purchased our freedom by his own blood, and there must be no returning to former "lovers". There is also an example here of the preliminaries which must precede the re-fellowshipping of any who having left the faith wish to return. Only after a period in which they have proved their repentance to be genuine should they be invited to break bread with us.

We now pass from the real life parable to that which it represents; from Gomer to Israel: "For the children of Israel shall abide many days without a king, and without a prince, and without a sacrifice, and without an image, and without an ephod, and without teraphim." It will be noted that the above list includes items from both true and false worship; as Gomer was to be without her lovers and for a period without Hosea, so Israel would abide for many days without either false gods or the true God. History has proved this to be true: the "many days" have become the long period in which the rebels are being purged out so that ultimately the remnant will emerge to seek the Lord their God (v. 5).

The reader will already have noticed how Hosea shows God to have a purpose within a purpose. Firstly there is the overall plan which offers redemption to the whole of mankind, Jew and Gentile alike, through the sacrifice of our Lord Jesus Christ; then there is another purpose which deals with Israel as a nation. Whilst Hosea is really only concerned with Israel (the ten tribes) he does also mention Judah (the two tribes) whose wickedness, though not so developed as that of Israel, is nevertheless such that it is only a matter of time before they too are taken into captivity. The regathering is therefore a regathering of a remnant from the whole of the *twelve* tribes who will then form one nation in the land of Israel, having one king and being the centre of all nations during the millennial age. So Hosea writes: "Afterward shall the children of Israel return, and seek the LORD their God, and David their king."

The name David is used of the Lord Jesus; its meaning *beloved* is used poetically of Jesus throughout the Song of Solomon. God also declares Jesus to be His "beloved Son" at both his baptism and transfiguration. He is the one who will be sought by Israel *and* Judah (cf. Jeremiah 50:4 and Ezekiel 37:22).

4

"THE LORD HATH A CONTROVERSY"
VERSES 1,2

*H*EAR *the word of the* LORD, *ye children of Israel: for the* LORD *hath a controversy with the inhabitants of the land, because there is no truth, nor mercy, nor knowledge of God in the land.*

2 By swearing, and lying, and killing, and stealing, and committing adultery, they break out, and blood toucheth blood.

WITH the commencement of this chapter we leave the real life parable. God no longer speaks to Israel through the figure of Hosea's broken marriage. Instead His condemnation is forthright and it exposes the utter depravity of Israel: " . . . there is no truth, nor mercy, nor knowledge of God in the land. By swearing, and lying, and killing, and stealing, and committing adultery, they break out, and blood toucheth blood."

We are able to learn much more about sin from these verses than a first reading might suggest. Not only did they lack knowledge but they were also murderously violent, so much so that Hosea may well have feared for his life. During Hosea's ministry no fewer than seven kings occupied the throne of Israel; blood flowed like water and this lack of stability in high places led to an insecure priesthood and the consequent lack of knowledge amongst the people.

The first verse makes it abundantly clear that this was not merely a lack of ordinary knowledge—it was a lack of knowledge about God and therefore there was no truth or mercy in the land. At the commencement of his Gospel, John gives to us what may be seen as an analysis of God's glory—it is "grace and truth" (John 1:14). These same qualities are to be seen in the name by which God chose to introduce Himself to Israel, and which is always represented in the Authorized Version as "LORD". To have knowledge of God is to understand how by a marriage of "mercy" and "truth", God is able to save—to the uttermost!

The basis of the Lord's controversy is that Israel has departed from Him. They have so neglected Him that it is written, "There is no knowledge of God in the land", and without this knowledge and its cleansing influence, human nature has run riot. God speaking through Jeremiah says: "For my people have committed two evils; they have forsaken me the fountain of living waters, and hewed them out cisterns, broken cisterns, that can hold no water" (2:13). When man departs from God, not only does he forsake the One who can save him but he further destroys himself, by his own self-elected means.

We must not underestimate the fact that where people cease to think upon the mercy and truth of God, they exhibit precisely the opposite in their lives. They become men of deceit and violence. It is not that Israel had just ignored God's revelation of Himself, they had actually pursued an active course of wickedness as if they must disprove in their lives what they have mentally rejected. This attitude is a product of the human mind and we are counselled against it many times in the Scriptures. For example, we read in Matthew 12:43-44 of the man out of whom an evil spirit was cast, but in whom no fewer than seven subsequently made their home. And again in Hebrews 6:4-6: "For it is impossible for those who were once enlightened, and have tasted of the heavenly gift, and were made partakers of the Holy Spirit, and have tasted of the good word of God, and the powers of the world to come, if they shall fall away, to renew them again unto repentance." It seems as though the pendulum when once lifted and released must swing as far in the opposite direction, so the higher it has been lifted the further it will swing! The wickedness of those who fall from grace seems to know no bounds.

25

It is in this context that we must examine the word *controversy*. Initially it means that God had cause or reason to contend with Israel but in this most awful confrontation there is hope, for the word also means *pleading* and is in fact so translated in chapter 2, verse 2: "Plead with your mother, plead." This same sense comes out also in Jeremiah 25:31:

" . . . the Lord hath a controversy with the nations, he will plead with all flesh . . ."

This confrontation then, which spells disaster for all those who persist in their own ways, is also a means of hope for those who will listen—it is God, positively and purposefully pleading with man to change his way and to accept His salvation.

Whilst this controversy is with Israel, Judah is not left without warning (v. 15); unhappily the warning was not heeded, so we read in chapter 12, verse 2: "The Lord hath also a controversy with Judah." It was only a matter of time which separated Judah from the depravity of Israel.

"I WILL ALSO REJECT THEE"

VERSES 3-6

3 Therefore shall the land mourn, and every one that dwelleth therein shall languish, with the beasts of the field, and with the fowls of heaven; yea, the fishes of the sea also shall be taken away.

4 Yet let no man strive, nor reprove another: for thy people are as they that strive with the priest.

5 Therefore shalt thou also fall in the day, and the prophet also shall fall with thee in the night, and I will destroy thy mother.

6 My people are destroyed for lack of knowledge: because thou hast rejected knowledge, I will also reject thee, that thou shalt be no priest to me: seeing thou hast forgotten the law of thy God, I will also forget thy children.

Verse 3 takes us back to the desolation of the land of Israel, a desolation only fulfilled in part by what has already happened, but which will reach its climax just before the return of Jesus (cf. Zechariah 14:1-3; Joel 3:9-16, etc.). As the present fruitfulness of the land is only a foretaste of that which shall be, so the past desolation is only a shadow of the clouds yet to gather over the land.

Whilst it is true that God sought Israel's repentance, it is also true that He knew she would not repent. That generation had so rejected Him "that there was no healing for her bruise", to use an expression used in Scripture of Babylon. A remnant from subsequent generations would respond and benefit from the appeal but that generation would witness the awful finality of the words, "I will also reject thee".

There was little point in reproof (v. 4), the people had gone so far as to rebel against the priest. This was a sin so serious, that death was its prescribed penalty: "And the man that will do presumptuously, and will not hearken unto the priest that standeth to minister there before the LORD thy God, or unto the judge, even that man shall die: and thou shalt put away the evil from Israel" (Deuteronomy 17:12). The people would fall in the day and the prophets would fall with them in the night; but more awful still, God would destroy "their mother". This, as we have seen, was a figure used to represent the nation of Israel; although a remnant would be spared to preserve the representation of the ten tribes, the nation would be destroyed. Never again would the kingdom of the ten tribes exist. The people's self-inflicted ignorance and their positive rejection of the knowledge which saves, had rendered them unfit to be the kingdom of priests to which they had been called along with Judah (Exodus 19:5,6).

We read in the end of verse 6: " . . . seeing thou hast forgotten the law of thy God, I will also forget thy children." This is a salutary warning that children may very well suffer because of the folly of their parents. It is not that God specifically punishes children for the sins of their parents, rather that they are affected by the consequences of the behaviour of their parents. There is a relevant verse which is often misquoted in this connection: " . . . keeping mercy for thousands, forgiving iniquity and transgression and sin, and that will by no means clear the guilty; visiting the iniquity of the fathers upon the children, and upon the children's children, unto the third and to the fourth generation" (Exodus 34:7). The words are often misused in an attempt to prove that God specifically punishes children for the sins of their parents, whilst what is actually being said is that God is abundant in grace and truth, that He does forgive iniquity, transgression and sin—but that he will not clear the guilty. Instead He will see that justice is done in them and will witness the consequences of their folly working itself out in their children and their children's children. The word "visiting" means *to look over*—God will witness or look over the affairs of men and see this truth fulfilled.

Children are to a large degree imprisoned in the life style chosen by their parents. What we choose for ourselves will so often determine what our children will become. It would appear that Timothy's faith began with the pattern set by his grandmother and maintained by his mother (2 Timothy 1:5), whilst on the other hand it may very well have been David's own weakness regarding women which led to such disastrous results in the lives of his sons Solomon and Amnon. It is left to very few children to rise above their environment as did Ruth, who though a member of a cursed race which was banned for ever from the congregation of the Lord (Deuteronomy 23:3), did nevertheless succeed in becoming a progenitor of the Lord Jesus Christ. Experience also shows that what may only be a temporary lapse for the parents, very often has permanently damaging results in the lives of their children.

God had purposely commanded His people to instruct their children in His ways: "And these words, which I command thee this day, shall be in thine heart: and thou shalt teach them diligently unto thy children, and shalt talk of them when thou sittest in thine house, and when thou walkest by the way, and when thou liest down, and when thou risest up. And thou shalt bind them for a sign upon thine hand, and they shall be as frontlets between thine eyes"

(Deuteronomy 6:6-8). But a generation had arisen which had rejected the knowledge given to them and because of this were in no position to teach their children. Although they had been selected to be custodians of God's word they were not able to teach their children. Even worse, they had little desire to do so!

"THE PEOPLE THAT DOTH NOT UNDERSTAND SHALL FALL"
VERSES 7-14

7 As they were increased, so they sinned against me: therefore will I change their glory into shame.

8 They eat up the sin of my people, and they set their heart on their iniquity.

9 And there shall be, like people, like priest: and I will punish them for their ways, and reward them their doings.

10 For they shall eat, and not have enough: they shall commit whoredom, and shall not increase: because they have left off to take heed to the LORD.

11 Whoredom and wine and new wine take away the heart.

12 My people ask counsel at their stocks, and their staff declareth unto them: for the spirit of whoredoms hath caused them to err, and they have gone a whoring from under their God.

13 They sacrifice upon the tops of the mountains, and burn incense upon the hills, under oaks and poplars and elms, because the shadow thereof is good: therefore your daughters shall commit whoredom, and your spouses shall commit adultery.

14 I will not punish your daughters when they commit whoredom, nor your spouses when they commit adultery: for themselves are separated with whores, and they sacrifice with harlots: therefore the people that doth not understand shall fall.

A knowledge of the Word of God not only makes a man wise unto salvation, it also furnishes him unto all good works; it instructs him in doctrine, convicts him of errors and provides the necessary correction to keep him on the right path (2 Timothy 3:16,17). To lack this knowledge is to be left a prey to delusions of all kinds, but wilfully to reject it is to set in motion all the human forces of self-destruction. The way of life which the people have chosen is seen to take away their "heart" or, as the Revised Version expresses it, their "understanding" (v. 11).

They are now void of judgement, void of the ability rightly to assess, being instead dominated by the "heart of man which is deceitful above all things, and desperately wicked". To forsake God is to forsake the only source of power which can deal with the human mind; it is to capitulate to all the evil forces of human nature. This is seen to be a vicious circle as the people, having been destroyed by their whoredoms, now seek advice from the very idols which they have chosen (v. 12).

The lesson must not be missed. Having neglected God who could have saved them, they compounded their folly by seeking guidance from the blind! How could they expect to obtain light from darkness? Like the prodigal son who left his father's house and later joined himself to a citizen of a far-off country so that his wants might be satisfied, but to his sorrow found himself still wanting even the husks which the swine did eat, so Israel were in want. But unlike the prodigal they did not know it!

The delusion caused by the deceitful heart of man upsets true judgement; the real source of blessing is no longer acknowledged (2:8) and those blessings are used to multiply sin (v. 7). A tendency is developed to "heap to themselves teachers having itching ears", to cease to seek sound doctrine and instead to fashion their teachers in their own image: "There shall be, like people, like priest" (v. 9). The whole cycle moves them swiftly to destruction whilst they live in ignorance of their true position.

This pathway has only one end, and the route is both circuitous and painful. Of that generation God said, "I will turn their glory

30

into shame" (v. 7). In this connection we can contrast the glory of the kingdom as it was in the days of Solomon, with the vision seen by Malachi: "Therefore have I also made you contemptible and base before all the people, according as ye have not kept my ways, but have been partial in the law" (2:9). Their spirit of whoredom is followed by their daughters (v. 13) and there is no need for God to punish them, for without understanding they will fall (v. 14). They have separated themselves; they have chosen to follow the example of their parents, and with them they must perish.

"YET LET NOT JUDAH OFFEND"
VERSES 15-19

> 15 Though thou, Israel, play the harlot, yet let not Judah offend; and come not ye unto Gilgal, neither go ye up to Beth-aven, nor swear, The LORD liveth.
> 16 For Israel slideth back as a backsliding heifer: now the LORD will feed them as a lamb in a large place.
> 17 Ephraim is joined to idols: let him alone.
> 18 Their drink is sour: they have committed whoredom continually: her rulers with shame do love, Give ye.
> 19 The wind hath bound her up in her wings, and they shall be ashamed because of their sacrifices.

The dire consequences of Israel's waywardness should have been a sufficient warning to Judah not to follow in her steps, but this was not so (Jeremiah 3:8). The remaining verses of this chapter, therefore, contain God's direct warning to Judah and through them to all who will listen to the counsel. To see the full import of the message we shall first examine the background to the place names which are introduced.

"Come not ye unto Gilgal." Gilgal was the place where the children of Israel set up their first camp on entering the land promised to their fathers (Joshua 4:19). In compliance with God's

31

command they had fulfilled a type of baptism. Twelve stones had been carried into the midst of Jordan and left there (Joshua 4:9) to mark the end of their old life—just as the slain Egyptians had marked the end of their fathers' experiences as they were baptized "in the cloud and in the sea" (1 Corinthians 10:2)—and twelve *fresh* stones were taken up from the bed of the Jordan and used to build an altar in the new land (v. 20). This was the baptism of a new generation which had been born in the wilderness and which was subsequently circumcised to confirm the rolling away of the old life (Joshua 5:4). It was also at this first possession in the land that they kept the first Passover (Joshua 5:10) and where Joshua was made to understand that to receive God's protection he must walk in God's way. An angel with a drawn sword appeared to him and their brief conversation is recorded in Joshua 5:13-15: "Joshua went unto him, and said unto him, Art thou for us, or for our adversaries? and he said, Nay; but as captain of the host of the LORD am I now come." It was Joshua who had to decide upon which side *he* stood.

It was also from Gilgal that an angel visited the next generation warning of the need for separation (Judges 2:1). From this incident we learn that Joshua's generation had failed in their duty to teach their children: "And there arose another generation after them, who knew not the LORD, nor yet the works which he had done for Israel" (v. 10). In addition it will be remembered that Gilgal was in the ministerial circuit of Samuel (1 Samuel 7:16) and it was there that Israel's first human king was crowned (1 Samuel 11:15).

Gilgal was therefore a landmark in both Israel's historical and religious development and had much to do with their birth as a nation. But alas, in the days of Hosea these things were of little importance to the people: "All their wickedness is in Gilgal: for there I hated them: for the wickedness of their doings I will drive them out of my house, I will love them no more: all their princes are revolters" (Hosea 9:15). Not being satisfied with their rejection of God, they must also desecrate His house with their merchandise!

The sin of the desecration of the things which are at the heart of our salvation is equally a sin whether it is blatant or the result of subtle intrusion. Whilst we do not have buildings or places of special significance to desecrate as had Israel, we do well to examine the structure of our ecclesial activities from time to time and to ask ourselves such questions as, What is the real purpose of this? Does it really lead to a fuller understanding of the kingdom of God and His righteousness or is it a concession to worldliness? Do our various ecclesial activities represent cameos of the family of God?

Though Israel plays the harlot and introduces her many lovers into the presence of her "husband", Judah do not thou offend! Maintain the necessary holiness of the things which belong to God. "Neither go ye up to Beth-aven" (house of wickedness): this name is introduced ironically in contrast with "Beth-el" (house of God). Bethel was the place to which the patriarchs often returned to renew their strength and sometimes their direction. It had special association with the presence of God as is seen from the following representative verses: Genesis 31:13; 35:1,3,6,8,15. Now they used God's name only in their blasphemies—"the Lord liveth"—and no place retained its holiness. Israel provides a warning for all time against using God's name lightly and profaning His house.

"For Israel slideth back as a backsliding heifer." The Revised Version uses a different translation: " . . . hath behaved himself stubbornly, like a stubborn heifer." This leads us to a verse in Deuteronomy, where the word is so used (21:20). The verse speaks of a stubborn son who would not listen to his father and for whom the only course of action was that he should be stoned. How ironical, that, like the heifer, Israel should, whilst thinking itself to be moving forwards, actually be sliding backwards and doing so to certain destruction.

It is a sad and dreadful picture of Israel which is contained in the last verse. Israel, previously described under the poetic name of "Ephraim" (*doubly fruitful*) has now come to the end, having wasted her fruitfulness in idol worship. The carousel is over! Their drink is sour! Judah is counselled to "let him alone". Israel has passed any hope of redemption and lest Judah should be defiled, he

33

is counselled to maintain a rigid separation. Excommunication is a very serious step, but it is far more serious to allow profanity to stay and corrupt that which remains.

5

"A SNARE ON MIZPAH"
VERSES 1-9

*H*EAR *ye this, O priests; and hearken, ye house of
Israel; and give ye ear, O house of the king; for
judgment is toward you, because ye have been a snare
on Mizpah, and a net spread upon Tabor.*

*2 And the revolters are profound to make slaughter,
though I have been a rebuker of them all.*

*3 I know Ephraim, and Israel is not hid from me: for
now, O Ephraim, thou committest whoredom, and Israel
is defiled.*

*4 They will not frame their doings to turn unto their
God: for the spirit of whoredoms is in the midst of them,
and they have not known the* LORD.

*5 And the pride of Israel doth testify to his face:
therefore shall Israel and Ephraim fall in their iniquity;
Judah also shall fall with them.*

*6 They shall go with their flocks and with their herds
to seek the* LORD*; but they shall not find him; he hath
withdrawn himself from them.*

7 They have dealt treacherously against the LORD*: for
they have begotten strange children: now shall a month
devour them with their portions.*

*8 Blow ye the cornet in Gibeah, and the trumpet in
Ramah: cry aloud at Beth-aven, after thee, O Benjamin.*

*9 Ephraim shall be desolate in the day of rebuke:
among the tribes of Israel have I made known that which
shall surely be.*

35

THE section which begins with chapter 4:1 and continues through to chapter 6:3, reaches a climax at the end of chapter 5, in which God, having pleaded with both Israel and Judah, is seen to leave them until they seek Him in their affliction. Since that generation did not return to seek the Lord, we must see the message as having continuing value to the "remnant", right up to the establishment of the kingdom of God.

Therefore we see in the details which are added in this chapter to fill out the picture of Israel's sins and of God's method of handling them, details from which lessons can be drawn for all time. The chapter opens with a condemnation which covers the whole kingdom—the priests, the house of Israel and the king's house. All had been guilty of falsehood. They had been a snare upon "Mizpah" (watch tower)—this was the place where Laban had called upon God to be a witness between Jacob and himself, to watch over their loyalty to each other when they were apart, and as such the name stands for the committing of their behaviour to the witness of the ever watching God. This covenant Israel had turned into a snare and they had spread a net upon "Tabor"—one of their high places. There was nothing but corruption from top to bottom, from priest to people, from king to commoner.

Despite God's continued rebuke, the nation had revolted and was now deeply involved in slaughter (v. 2). The spirit which causes division is always self-destructive and those who had divided what had been God's kingdom were now to be found slaying each other. Those who had been disloyal to their king could find no loyalty amongst themselves. The spirit of division bears the fruits of bitterness and strife which "eats as doth a canker", until those who have caused division shrivel to a mere shadow of their former selves. So the apostle Paul counsels: "Now I beseech you, brethren, mark them which cause divisions and offences contrary to the doctrine which ye have learned; and avoid them. For they that are such serve not our Lord Jesus Christ" (Romans 16:17).

From those who have received special instruction and remedial rebuke much is expected; the grace of God leads to greater responsibility and therefore to more severe judgement. This was to be Israel's experience, but we do well to remember that this principle did not end with Israel. God's final judgements will begin at the household of faith.

Although it was written of Israel, "They have not known me" (v. 4), God makes it quite clear that He had known them: "I know Ephraim" (v. 3). He knew all the circumstances and saw through all the excuses used to justify their "strange" way of life. He knows whether one is joined together with Him in faithfulness, or is in practice "joined to an idol". It is impossible to be joined to both since such would involve God in idolatry! To take up the teaching of Jesus on this matter: "You cannot serve God and mammon."

Israel was completely captivated by "the spirit of whoredoms" (v. 4); the very essence of their lives was with strange gods. The use of the word "spirit" in the Scriptures is such that it describes the essence of the life to which it refers. Thus when speaking of the spirit of man it is coupled with such words as lust, disobedience, pride, envy, whoredoms etc., but when used in reference to God the list of words is quite different: holiness, love, joy, peace, compassion. Thus the things which dominate the life of man reveal his spirit and in Ephraim it was "whoredoms", their continual union with idolatry. This had destroyed their knowledge of God and caused "their pride" or their excellence to testify against them (v. 5).

When certain Greeks said, "We would see Jesus" and the message was passed to him, his answer was: "If any man serve me, let him follow me; and where I am, there shall also my servant be" (John 12:26). This was a clear statement that he is to be found in service, by those who labour with him. The same advice was given to the maiden who was seeking the one whom she loved (Song of Solomon 1:7,8): "If thou know not, O thou fairest among women, go thy way forth by the footsteps of the flock, and feed thy kids beside the shepherds' tents". She must go and feed her kids where both he and his flock are to be found. The children of Israel now follow this advice, but it is too late; the day of opportunity has passed: "They shall go with their flocks and with their herds to seek the LORD; but they shall not find him; he hath withdrawn himself from them" (v. 6).

Having failed to grasp the opportunity whilst they could have done so, their hearts have now become treacherous (v. 7) and their way of life such that they had brought forth "strange children". This was a reference to the children of the real life parable, made here to emphasise that the fruits of their lives were corrupt. Having destroyed themselves, repentance was no longer possible. Furthermore, God had withdrawn Himself from them. They would blow their trumpet in vain (v. 8). The treachery of "Gibeah", which exposed the weakness of Benjamin and saw the death of some 25,000 of his trained men in one day (Judges 19 & 20) had remained with them: "They have deeply corrupted themselves, as in the day of Gibeah" (9:9); "O, Israel, thou hast sinned from the days of Gibeah" (10:9).

Ephraim was to be made desolate and the people were without excuse; not only had God sought to save them, He had also given adequate warning of the consequences of disobedience: "Among the tribes of Israel have I made known that which shall surely be" (v. 9). No other decisions in life are so clearly defined as are those which affect our salvation and yet how often we choose the wrong things! In matters of business or domestic crisis, man can only make a calculated guess at the outcome of his actions, but in all matters where God is concerned everything is detailed. The issues are clearly stated. The right advice is given. The blessings of the right course are temptingly portrayed, whilst the consequences of taking the wrong action are stated in language which strikes terror to the heart. Yet man still chooses to go the wrong way!

Such blatant folly can only result in utter desolation. Of Ephraim to whom God had made His way known, it was said: "Ephraim shall be desolate" (v. 9); and with searching words Isaiah speaks to "everyone that thirsteth": "Wherefore do ye spend money for that which is not bread? and your labour for that which satisfieth not? hearken diligently unto me, and eat ye that which is good, and let your soul delight itself in fatness" (Isaiah 55:1,2).

"I WILL GO AND RETURN TO MY PLACE"

VERSES 10-15

10 The princes of Judah were like them that remove the bound: therefore I will pour out my wrath upon them like water.

11 Ephraim is oppressed and broken in judgment, because he willingly walked after the commandment.

12 Therefore will I be unto Ephraim as a moth, and to the house of Judah as rottenness.

13 When Ephraim saw his sickness, and Judah saw his wound, then went Ephraim to the Assyrian, and sent to king Jareb: yet could he not heal you, nor cure you of your wound.

14 For I will be unto Ephraim as a lion, and as a young lion to the house of Judah: I, even I, will tear and go away; I will take away, and none shall rescue him.

15 I will go and return to my place, till they acknowledge their offence, and seek my face: in their affliction they will seek me early.

These verses speak of the certainty of repentance: "In their hour of affliction they will seek me early" (earnestly). But since, as we have already noted, that generation did not repent, the words must be prophetic of the penitence of a people yet to come. Therefore the latter part of this chapter may be seen as an exhortation for all who would seek God's kingdom and His righteousness.

It may be helpful to note that there are two lines of thought running side by side through these verses which may be considered separately. They are (a) God's method of dealing with sinners, and (b) the specific sins of Israel and Judah which led to their rejection and which in principle are common to all men.

The outline of God's method is really an expansion of that which was seen in chapter 2, verses 6, 9 and 14, and its introduction here provides another example of God's method of teaching by a system of gentle repetition, with the introduction of new material in a way which can be easily understood and assimilated.

1. Firstly, God makes His purpose known (v. 9). In this way He not only invites repentance but He also leaves those who do not do so entirely without excuse. The apostle Paul makes a similar point when writing to the church at Rome: "For the invisible things of him from the creation of the world are clearly seen, being understood by the things that are made . . . so that they are without excuse" (1:20).

2. After knowledge comes responsibility: "I will pour out my wrath upon them like water" (v. 10) and as with the flood which covered "every high hill under heaven", none can escape the wrath of God. The flood was, however, both a deluge unto death and a baptism unto salvation (1 Peter 3:20,21). Similarly God's forewarning of His judgements which will separate the wheat from the chaff, is man's opportunity (Malachi 4:1,2; Matthew 13:41-43).

3. The outpouring of God's wrath is preceded by remedial affliction which is seen first as "a moth" and "rottenness" (v. 12). The slow decay of the nation should have been sufficient to have turned them back to their God but since this failed, a more stringent step was taken.

4. "For I will be unto Ephraim as a lion, and as a young lion to the house of Judah: I, even I, will tear and go away; I will take away, and none shall rescue him" (v. 14). God judged His people through the fierceness of their enemies who tore them without mercy. The prophet Amos underlines this same method of handling sinful Israel: "I have smitten you with blasting and mildew . . . yet ye have not returned unto me . . . prepare to meet thy God, O Israel" (4:9-12). Clearly, the tribulation was intended to be remedial; thus the sin of rejection brought greater judgement upon them.

5. Having reduced Israel to utter helplessness, God awaits the acknowledgement of their offences. The history of Israel has shown this stage to be both fierce and long: all can witness the

beginning of the truth of the words spoken through the prophet
Ezekiel: "As I live, saith the Lord GOD, surely with a mighty
hand, and with a stretched out arm, and with fury poured out,
will I rule over you . . . And I will bring you into the wilderness
of the people, and there will I plead with you face to face . . .
and I will purge out from among you the rebels . . . and ye shall
know that I am the LORD" (20:33-38).

Such were God's acts of remedial chastisement, applicable to
Israel, but typifying God's great work of redemption for all. We
shall now consider that generation's reaction to this chastisement,
seeing how easily they were deluded and why God had to cut them
off. The people of God will be ever watchful for such illustrations
which may help them to succeed where Israel failed.

1. "The princes of Judah were like them that remove the bound"
   (v. 10): they were guilty of removing the landmarks, a heinous
   offence under the Law (Deuteronomy 19:14). The priesthood
   had been persecuted, God's law had been subdued and perverted
   and without this necessary guidance their lives were purposeless
   and they themselves an easy prey to the lusts of human nature.
   As we read in Ecclesiastes: "Whoso breaketh an hedge, a ser-
   pent shall bite him. Whoso removeth stones shall be hurt
   therewith" (10:8,9). There can be no substitute for God's laws,
   no other foundation can be laid than that which has been laid (1
   Corinthians 3:11), therefore to tamper with the fundamentals of
   our faith is to court disaster.

2. "He willingly walked after the commandment" (v. 11). The
   people were not coerced into idolatry, they went willingly. Of
   their own free will they responded to the command of Jeroboam:
   "Behold thy gods, O Israel, which brought thee up out of the
   land of Egypt" (1 Kings 12:28). To be guilty of wilful rebellion
   against the laws of God is to be guilty of the sin for which there
   is no forgiveness (Hebrews 10:26). It is important, however,
   that we differentiate between the sins which we commit through
   weakness, even though we know such to be wrong, and the blatant sins which are committed in the spirit of 'I know this is

41

wrong, but I don't care!' For the former there can be forgiveness, but the latter displays an arrogance and wilful disobedience to God which puts one beyond His far-reaching mercy.

3. "When Ephraim saw his sickness, and Judah saw his wound, then went Ephraim to the Assyrian, and sent to king Jareb" (v. 13). The whole purpose of Israel's humiliation was that they should turn to and trust in their God who had delivered them from their enemies of the past. But in their weakness they sought the worthless help of Assyria. They were sadly let down. What help can be given to a man who persists in seeking help from the very source of his trouble?

4. "I will go and return to my place" (v. 15). For God to *return* to His place, He must first have been with Israel, but unrecognised. He must have been with her in all her tribulation. From the day when He had said to Moses, "I am come down to deliver", God had been closely involved with the lives of His people and never was this more true than in the last days of the dying kingdom. It was His intention "to speak to her heart" (2:14, R.V. margin), to give her every opportunity to repent.

Having done all that was possible, God withdrew Himself to await Israel's response, but it was a response which He knew would only come from the "remnant". There is no doubt that God is preserving a remnant from among the children of Israel and that they will be exalted once more to be above all nations. But what is of greater importance to us, is that a people is being gathered from all nations and throughout all ages, a people born out of "great tribulation" and having "washed their robes and made them white in the blood of the lamb", a people delivered through the same principles of salvation as were revealed to Israel of old. Unlike that generation, however, they will have "acknowledged their offences" and sought God "earnestly". They will have come to realise how easily man is deluded into thinking his strength lies in success in this life and that such blessings as are temptingly offered are very temporary. They will have sought first the kingdom of God and His righteousness.

6

"COME, AND LET US RETURN UNTO THE LORD"
VERSES 1-3

*C*OME, and let us return unto the LORD: for he
hath torn, and he will heal us; he hath smitten, and
he will bind us up.

*2 After two days will he revive us: in the third day he
will raise us up, and we shall live in his sight.*

*3 Then shall we know, if we follow on to know the
LORD: his going forth is prepared as the morning; and
he shall come unto us as the rain, as the latter and former
rain unto the earth.*

THE previous chapter closes with God having done all that was
possible to redeem His people and then having withdrawn to
await their repentance. It is almost as though, limited by the
parameters of His own plan of salvation, God could do no more
until Israel responded; and that in the interim Israel was "without
God in the world", the beginning of a tragic fulfilment of the
prophecy of chapter 3, verses 4 and 5. Is it true to say, however,
that God was powerless to help further until Israel repented, that He
could do no more for them until they sought Him?

It is certainly true that God had already done much for Israel—
remedial chastisement, compassionate pleading and above all in the
paying of the price of their freedom from slavery. But even after
all this He has not yet finished! His work of redemption still goes
on, as is to be seen in this chapter. Israel must repent before she
can be forgiven, but there is much more that God can and will do.

Although Gomer is not mentioned after chapter 3, much of the appeal of this prophecy is lost if the reader fails to see her relationship with Hosea as a background to all the remaining chapters. Although the message is directed to the ten tribes, we must remember that it is a message for us through their experiences; its real fulfilment is to make "sons of the living God" (1:10; Romans 9:26). The spirit of Christ which was in the prophets is speaking to us (1 Peter 1:10-12). God has returned to His place but He has not left Himself without witness nor us without the urgency of His message. This chapter opens with an appeal to join with the one who was smitten, that with him we may be healed: "Come, and let us return unto the LORD: for he hath torn, and he will heal us; he hath smitten, and he will bind us up."

Hosea would gather together into the experiences of God's only begotten Son all who will listen; and the words are really the words of Jesus, who on God's behalf makes this impassioned plea that we might gather together the consequences of this remedial chastisement into the light of his cross. God has torn but He will heal; He has smitten but He will also bind up and even more we shall share in Christ's resurrection on the third day. It is the spirit of Christ in the prophet which anticipates the well known words: "Come unto me, all ye that labour and are heavy laden, and I will give you rest" (Matthew 11:28-30); it is an invitation to share in his death that we might "live in his sight" (v. 2).

This hope can only be shared by those who are prepared to "return unto the Lord", those who will recognise that from the day of Adam man has been walking in darkness—the darkness of the shadow of his own presence as he walks away from God. The hope is for those who will turn round to face God, who can be seen in the one who was sent to bear His image, the manifestation of His glory, and whose spirit speaks through the prophets. The Apostle John captures this same theme in a sequence of verses in which he writes of the manifestation of God in Jesus:

1 John 1:2   "The life was manifested in Jesus"

1 John 3:5   "The Son was manifested to take away sins"

1 John 3:8	"The Son of God was manifested to destroy the works of the devil"
1 John 4:9	"The love of God was manifested that we might live through his Son"

Hosea continues by speaking of the blessing which will follow those who return to God: "Then shall we know" (v. 3). Submission to the will of God is the beginning of rebirth; ignorance will be turned to knowledge, darkness into light, or as James writes: "Humble yourselves in the sight of the Lord, and he shall lift you up" (4:10). Feet will be set on a new path which must then be trodden in a state of contrition, for repentance is not the act of a moment; the penitent must "follow on to know the LORD" (v. 3).

The Messianic teaching of these verses takes us once more into the kingdom of God: "His going forth is prepared (sure, R.V.) as the morning; and he shall come unto us as the rain." Here is the substance of many memorable prayers and prophecies: "He shall come."

Genesis 49:10	"Until Shiloh come"
Isaiah 35:4	"He will come and save you"
Isaiah 40:10	"The Lord GOD will come . . . his reward is with him"
Isaiah 59:20	"The Redeemer shall come to Zion"

He will come "as the rain" and will rain righteousness upon those who have broken up their fallow ground (10:12). There is no doubt that he will come. The doubt is whether he will find faith in the earth.

"FOR I DESIRED MERCY, AND NOT SACRIFICE"
VERSES 4-11

4 O Ephraim, what shall I do unto thee? O Judah, what shall I do unto thee? for your goodness is as a morning cloud, and as the early dew it goeth away.

5 Therefore have I hewed them by the prophets; I have slain them by the words of my mouth: and thy judgments are as the light that goeth forth.

6 For I desired mercy, and not sacrifice; and the knowledge of God more than burnt offerings.

7 But they like men have transgressed the covenant: there have they dealt treacherously against me.

8 Gilead is a city of them that work iniquity, and is polluted with blood.

9 And as troops of robbers wait for a man, so the company of priests murder in the way by consent: for they commit lewdness.

10 I have seen an horrible thing in the house of Israel: there is the whoredom of Ephraim, Israel is defiled.

11 Also, O Judah, he hath set an harvest for thee, when I returned the captivity of my people.

Having been given a glimpse of the kingdom, we are taken back once more to consider the sins of Israel from yet another angle. This is a short section but the lessons are of extreme importance to those who would be numbered amongst "the sons of the living God".

Each section reminds us of the wonder of God's abounding mercy as He offers salvation to a worthless people, and such words as those of Isaiah 65:1-4 are made to live again:

"I am sought of them that asked not for me; I am found of them that sought me not: I said, Behold me, behold me, unto a nation that was not called by my name. I have spread out my hands all the day unto a rebellious people, which walketh in a way that was not good, after their own thoughts; a people that provoketh me to anger continually to my face; that sacrificeth in gardens, and burneth incense upon altars of brick; which remain among the graves, and lodge in the monuments, which eat swine's flesh, and broth of abominable things is in their vessels."

This time Judah does not escape condemnation: together with Israel he is roundly condemned. All their early promise has disappeared as the "morning cloud", their goodness has vanished as the "early dew" (v. 4). Against the background of Gomer's broken covenant, the people are condemned for "dealing treacherously", and like "Adam" for having transgressed the covenant (v. 7, R.V.). Gilead, known for its medicinal balm (Jeremiah 8:22), was polluted with blood and was a stronghold of iniquity. The priests, deprived of their living, no longer spoke out against the sin of murder and were implicated and guilty of gross indecency. Gomer's behaviour testifies against them; there is "an horrible thing in the house of Israel: there is the whoredom of Ephraim, Israel is defiled" (v. 10). "O Ephraim, what shall I do unto thee? O Judah, what shall I do unto thee" (v. 4).

The answer to the question follows without hesitation. "Therefore have I hewed them by the prophets: I have slain them by the words of my mouth: and thy judgments are as the light that goeth forth" (v. 5). Although God desires their salvation and rains remedial chastisement upon them, He remains true to His word. There can be no compromise with evil. All must see that none can flout His terms of forgiveness and live. His judgement upon Israel must go forth as a light; has He not said, "Ye are my witnesses"?

As a nation they were lifted up to be His bride, but they forsook Him, going in search of other husbands; now the world must know that although God is a God of love, He is also a God of truth—they must ever remain His witnesses.

There is a verse in the middle of this section which shines as a beacon, a verse which shows that God is not just exposing the sins of Israel but is also drawing out a lesson which is basic to His plan of salvation and as such relevant to all people: "For I desired mercy, and not sacrifice; and the knowledge of God more than burnt offerings."

We must not be led astray by a superficial reading of this verse: that would be to share in Israel's offence. God is not setting up mercy and sacrifice as opposites. He is not condemning the offering of sacrifices, but He is exposing their attitude of mind in the

47

offering thereof. Their worship was hollow, without heart; they were, as Malachi so clearly stated, guilty of robbing God whilst in the very act of offering sacrifices to Him (Malachi 3:7-12). They were going through the motions of seeking forgiveness, for God had given to them the blood of animals "upon the altar to make an atonement for your souls" (Leviticus 17:11), but there was no appreciation of His mercy and consequently no spilling over of that mercy from their own lives. There was no knowledge of God, no fear of His presence; their lives were filled with self.

This is a searching exhortation: to be exposed to the possibility of incurring condemnation whilst in the act of performing that which was designed to save. Is this not the Old Testament counterpart of, "Wherefore whosoever shall eat this bread, and drink this cup of the Lord, unworthily, shall be guilty of the body and blood of the Lord. But let a man examine himself, and so let him eat of that bread, and drink of that cup. For he that eateth and drinketh unworthily, eateth and drinketh damnation to himself, not discerning the Lord's body" (1 Corinthians 11:27-29)? How important it is then, that we should have a "knowledge of God", a knowledge of His redeeming mercy and of His searching truth and that these should be discerned along with the Lord's body in the emblems given for that purpose.

The prophet Micah takes up this same theme: "He hath showed thee, O man, what is good; and what doeth the Lord require of thee, but to do justly, and to love mercy, and to walk humbly with thy God?" It is not just that God has spoken; He has shown to us what is required! The word has been made flesh and in the life that was lived man has been shown how to "do justly and to love mercy". The miracle of the marriage of grace and truth has been revealed and it is the very basis of our salvation. Micah's words take us even further in our understanding. He adds: "Walk humbly with thy God." The Hebrew is literally, "Humble thyself to walk with thy God" as the margin of the Authorized Version shows. This suggests the humiliation experienced by God in His Son and teaches the remarkable fact that to walk with God, man must first be humble.

Any perfunctory performance which reduces righteousness to a mere ritual even though it may involve the God-given emblems of life, is a mere extension of self and by it man "eateth and drinketh damnation to himself". The ten tribes were defiled and doomed and even though God had "set an harvest" for Judah (v. 11), she would not see that harvest until she had first been "sown" amongst the nations. Before the captivity could return, it had first to be taken.

The harvest is certain, but it is not for those who defile their calling, whose "goodness is as a morning cloud" or who lack the real "knowledge of God".

7

"THE WICKEDNESS OF SAMARIA"
VERSES 1-16

*W*HEN *I would have healed Israel, then the iniquity of Ephraim was discovered, and the wickedness of Samaria: for they commit falsehood; and the thief cometh in, and the troop of robbers spoileth without.*

2 And they consider not in their hearts that I remember all their wickedness: now their own doings have beset them about; they are before my face.

3 They make the king glad with their wickedness, and the princes with their lies.

4 They are all adulterers, as an oven heated by the baker, who ceaseth from raising after he hath kneaded the dough, until it be leavened.

5 In the day of our king the princes have made him sick with bottles of wine; he stretched out his hand with scorners.

6 For they have made ready their heart like an oven, whiles they lie in wait: their baker sleepeth all the night; in the morning it burneth as a flaming fire.

7 They are all hot as an oven, and have devoured their judges; all their kings are fallen: there is none among them that calleth unto me.

8 Ephraim, he hath mixed himself among the people; Ephraim is a cake not turned.

9 Strangers have devoured his strength, and he knoweth it not: yea, gray hairs are here and there upon him, yet he knoweth not.

10 And the pride of Israel testifieth to his face: and they do not return to the LORD their God, nor seek him for all this.

11 Ephraim also is like a silly dove without heart: they call to Egypt, they go to Assyria.

12 When they shall go, I will spread my net upon
them; I will bring them down as the fowls of the heaven;
I will chastise them, as their congregation hath heard.
13 Woe unto them! for they have fled from me:
destruction unto them! because they have transgressed
against me: though I have redeemed them, yet they have
spoken lies against me.
14 And they have not cried unto me with their heart,
when they howled upon their beds: they assemble
themselves for corn and wine, and they rebel against me.
15 Though I have bound and strengthened their arms,
yet do they imagine mischief against me.
16 They return, but not to the most High: they are like
a deceitful bow: their princes shall fall by the sword for
the rage of their tongue: this shall be their derision in the
land of Egypt.

WE are not told of Gomer's response when Hosea sought her and bought her back, but it must have been in shame that she considered his action and in sorrow that she thought of her former way of life. It is true that she was not returned immediately to full marital status, but her feet were set on the path, and it is difficult to imagine that she would ever have thought to refuse Hosea's help; yet that was precisely what Israel did! It is the burden of this chapter to show Ephraim's constant refusal of God's help. It presents the incredible situation of a nation perishing in desperate need and refusing to accept the help which was so close to hand. In principle it represents the sad truth about human nature.

"When I would have healed Israel, then the iniquity of Ephraim was discovered, and the wickedness of Samaria." Ephraim is the poetic name for the ten tribes, meaning *doubly fruitful*, but Ephraim, like Gomer, who was the daughter of "fruitfulness", did not appreciate from whence her blessings came. So perverted was she that her very fruitfulness was the cause of her downfall—she "waxed fat, and kicked" (Deuteronomy 32:15). As with the whited sepulchres, behind Ephraim's exterior there was corruption. There is irony in the use of Samaria here: its meaning is *watch city*, but far from watching, the capital city of Israel presided over falsehood and violence; there were "thieves within and troops of robbers without". Worse still, they did not "consider in their hearts" that God remembered all their wickedness.

It was God's plan to heal that "discovered" Ephraim's iniquity. This is always the case. To be made aware of guilt is always the first step towards healing, but this awareness must be followed by an acknowledgement of the guilt and a pleading for forgiveness before that healing can follow. Of Israel we read, however: they "considered not in their hearts" that God knew and remembered their sins. There was no sense of God's presence, no thought of their own need, nor of the work in which God was involved to meet that need. Their sin was the unforgivable sin; they spurned God's offer of redemption: "He that despised Moses' law died without mercy under two or three witnesses: of how much sorer punishment, suppose ye, shall he be thought worthy, who hath trodden under foot the Son of God, and hath counted the blood of the covenant, wherewith he was sanctified, an unholy thing, and hath done despite unto the Spirit of grace?" (Hebrews 10:28,29). How complete is Hosea's summary: "And the pride of Israel testifieth to his face: and they do not return to the LORD their God, nor seek him for all this" (v. 10).

The same theme is taken up in verse 13 but, as we should expect, new points are introduced: "Though I would have redeemed them, yet have they spoken lies against me" (R.V.). Here we learn that Israel had "fled" or wandered away from God, and having turned her back upon His offer of redemption proceeded to speak lies against Him. If one refuses to accept God's salvation and turns away from Him, any attempt at self-justification must be built upon lies. Those who rejected Jesus had to fabricate false witness and so Israel added to her sin of rejection of God's salvation that of lies and falsehood. It is a sad fact that those who forsake the Truth, very often falsely condemn those whose fellowship they have left and a critical attitude towards brethren and sisters is often a warning that such a departure is near.

It will be remembered that as part of His plan of remedial chastisement, God said: "I will return, and take away my corn in the time thereof, and my wine in the season thereof" (2:9). In this chapter we see the people "assembling themselves for corn and wine" whilst at the same time rebelling against God. They refuse to see in God their provider and they "howl upon their beds" in their distress (v. 14). They refuse to confess unto God who could have saved and redeemed them and in self-justification invent lies about Him.

"They return, but not unto the most High." There is a kind of repentance but it is not genuine; there is some sort of recognition but it is a sham and they do not "return unto the most High". The people are frequently seen weeping and cutting themselves with knives, putting on sackcloth and covering themselves with ashes but there is no real heart to their repentance and they do not take their grief and their penitence to God. "They are like a deceitful bow" (v. 16) which will not shoot straight and which "misses the mark"; even in their hour of weeping there is sin. It is perhaps amongst the most difficult of things in our experience, to be able to recognise true repentance—even in ourselves; to differentiate between the sorrow of suffering and the sorrow of repentance, between the grief of isolation from brethren and sisters and the grief of an acknowledgement of separation from God. Perhaps the key question which should be asked when someone wishes to resume fellowship is, "Have you sought God's forgiveness?" since any reconciliation which ignores this is quite irrelevant. The wisdom of God's command that the children of Israel "should abide many days" before being united again to Him (3:4) is apparent here and should be used to help us to determine sincere repentance.

God's method of teaching by gentle repetition is very evident in Hosea's message. The main features—of Israel's weaknesses, of God's approaches to save, of Israel's rebellion and of the repeated glimpses of the Kingdom of God, are seen time and time again but always with the addition of something new. In this way the fundamental principles are made sure and our understanding of them is enlarged. In this chapter, the wickedness of Samaria is examined and four main aspects of it are set before us. Although they have specific reference to Israel, they are fundamental and as such are not without exhortational value to readers of all ages.

Firstly, the nation is seen to be like a baker's oven which has been built up, and although the fire is only smouldering, it will be stirred into a "flaming fire" when the dough is thoroughly leavened. It is a dreadful picture of the deceitful and wicked heart of man, of the leaven of wickedness and of how easily powers of destruction may be stirred up. The people have given way to their lusts which they are feeding instead of trying to subdue. They are habitual adulterers, in both literal and spiritual ways, and they scheme the downfall of their kings and princes. Verses 3-7 seem to be supplying the human background to the simple historical record of the slaying of the kings of Israel. Here we see drunkenness, debauchery and degenerate behaviour which result in the slaying of their kings and the fast decline of the nation. It is worth noting that division reduces, and the state of mind which first causes division continues to do so. Those who separate themselves continue to be divisive amongst themselves and, like Israel who separated from the two tribes but continued to destroy their self-elected kings, so modern separatist movements tend to devour themselves, shrinking smaller and smaller until they eventually disappear!

The people not only slay their kings, but also devour their judges. We have already seen how they brought down their priests to their own level (4:9), thus establishing their immorality. Now they remove their judges so that there is no remaining barrier to their wickedness. They have stirred up the heated oven of human nature and it devours the very structure of life which could have saved them.

Hosea points to a second weakness: "Ephraim, he hath mixed himself among the people" (v. 8). Since the time that God had called His people out of Egypt He had stressed the importance of separation. Theirs was a calling to a new and exalted way of life which could only be appreciated by leaving behind that from which they had been called. They were warned that any association with the nations around them would result in their becoming like them and in the loss of their many blessings. Note how Hosea spells this out as he marks each stage of decline.

They are as a "cake not turned", half-baked! They never reached the height of their calling; their failure to aspire to the new life and to be separate resulted in the loss of things both temporal and spiritual. Separation from the world from which we have been called is crucial to salvation, because it marks where our true interests are.

"Strangers have devoured his strength." The strangers amongst whom Israel mixed were responsible for devouring her strength! The very people to whom she went for help, robbed her of those things which remained. It is always the worldly things which sap our strength, the things which are not necessary to life for which people go into debt; and it is the things which are not of a spiritual nature which disrupt ecclesial life. Lack of separation from the world, whether it be in business, pleasure or general living results in loss of strength and the blessings which God had in store for us.

"Yet he knoweth not." Although in its dying years, the nation was like an ageing man who fails to recognise his grey hairs! It knew not; it was oblivious to what was happening! It was dying and yet did not know it! This is perhaps the greatest tragedy of sin—its consequences are not recognised by the sinner until it is too late. The only antidote is to live a separate life and continually use the mirror of Scripture. All other ways lead to obscurity as we adopt the likeness of those around and fail to see in that likeness the old man which should have been crucified with Christ.

Thirdly, Ephraim is seen as "a silly dove" (v. 11)—a bird without a homing instinct—going into Egypt and Assyria, but not returning to God. It is not without significance that the man Jonah, whose name means *dove*, failed to appreciate the principles of God's way of life and fled from his mission, to go instead into Tarshish. The lesson which Jonah was given was that there is forgiveness for all people if they will return to God. This Ephraim did not do.

Fourthly, we are brought again to the most amazing attitude which God displays in the face of all this rebellion: "When they shall go, I will spread my net upon them" (v. 12). As was seen in chapter 2, verse 7, this also is a remedial act. God will stop them in their tracks; He will catch them as in a net that He might bring them down to chastise them. In the face of destruction there is still hope if only they will heed God's hand and return to Him. This we shall never understand, but we shall always thank God that it is so—God is always ready to save those who seek Him. Alas, Ephraim did not return, and it is with sorrow, enriched by Hosea's own experiences with Gomer, that He says, "There is none among them that calleth unto me" (v. 7); "They do not return to the LORD their God, nor seek him for all this" (v. 10); "They have not cried unto me" (v. 14); and "They return, but not to the most High" (v. 16).

8

"THE HOUSE OF THE LORD"
VERSES 1-3

*S ET the trumpet to thy mouth. He shall come as an
eagle against the house of the LORD, because they
have transgressed my covenant, and trespassed against
my law.
2 Israel shall cry unto me, My God, we know thee.
3 Israel hath cast off the thing that is good: the enemy
shall pursue him.*

WHEN writing the letters to the seven churches, Jesus did not
describe them by the normal word for church but instead used
the word "ecclesia", thus giving his sanction to the apostles' use
of this term. The significance of this word is now well known,
drawing attention to the people who form the "church" rather than
to the building in which they meet. The same teaching is, however,
quite often missed when the Old Testament term "the house of the
Lord" is used, this usually being limited to the Temple. It is of
course true that the Temple was called the House of the Lord but
it is also true that God's people were God's House, and that the
Temple was a type of the Temple of people yet to be revealed, fitly
framed together and built upon the Lord Jesus Christ. It is this
understanding of the term "God's house", which helps us to
appreciate what is meant by the "many mansions" or "abiding
places" of which Jesus spoke (John 14:2).

Again, the Lord referred to Moses being faithful in all His house
(Numbers 12:7) and the apostle Paul used this quotation when
speaking of the house being built by Jesus, of which he says,
"Whose house are we, if we hold fast the confidence and the
rejoicing of the hope firm to the end" (Hebrews 3:1-6). God is concerned with people, not with buildings. This has always been the
case, even in Old Testament times, and the dual use of the term "the
house of the Lord" must be seen in verse 1 of this chapter.

The message of Hosea was in the first instance to the ten tribes who would be taken into captivity by Shalmaneser, but also included Judah, who would similarly be taken captive, though in their case by Nebuchadnezzar over 140 years later. The prophecy includes the destruction of the Temple and its being devoured by fire (v. 14). So both the people and their centre of worship were to experience the withdrawal of God's presence. Hosea's message was to go forth with the clarity of a trumpet call: the people had transgressed God's covenant, they had "cast off the thing that is good" and the enemy was to pursue them.

The time would come when Israel would cry unto God, saying, "My God, we know thee" (v. 2), but it would be in vain. As we have already seen, the people will not return unto God "with their hearts". They will cry in their affliction and they will seek to trade upon their special relationship with God, but since there will be no real penitence the crying will be in vain. There is a similar warning given to all disciples. Jesus says the time is coming when many will claim a special relationship with him but he will say, "I never knew you" (Matthew 7:23). Now is the time to get our own relationship right. Now is the time to recognise and confess our own weaknesses and to do so from the heart! Unless we do, there will be weeping and gnashing of teeth when God's judgements "begin at the house of God" (1 Peter 4:17).

"THEY HAVE SET UP KINGS, BUT NOT BY ME"
VERSES 4-11

4 They have set up kings, but not by me: they have made princes, and I knew it not: of their silver and their gold have they made them idols, that they may be cut off.

5 Thy calf, O Samaria, hath cast thee off; mine anger is kindled against them: how long will it be ere they attain to innocency?

6 For from Israel was it also: the workman made it; therefore it is not God: but the calf of Samaria shall be broken in pieces.

CHAPTER EIGHT

7 For they have sown the wind, and they shall reap the whirlwind: it hath no stalk: the bud shall yield no meal: if so be it yield, the strangers shall swallow it up.

8 Israel is swallowed up: now shall they be among the Gentiles as a vessel wherein is no pleasure.

9 For they are gone up to Assyria, a wild ass alone by himself: Ephraim hath hired lovers.

10 Yea, though they have hired among the nations, now will I gather them, and they shall sorrow a little for the burden of the king of princes.

11 Because Ephraim hath made many altars to sin, altars shall be unto him to sin.

Although Jeroboam was told by God that the kingdom was to be divided and that he would have ten tribes (1 Kings 11:13-37) and Rehoboam was told that the division was of the Lord (1 Kings 12:22-24), we must not lose sight of the fact that this happened because of the sins of Solomon (1 Kings 11:9-13). The division was a punishment which would defer the fulfilment of God's purpose. The behaviour of the ten tribes went even further to rouse God's anger. Their setting up of kings was not by God (v. 4). They did not commit their ways to Him, nor seek His guidance in the running of the newly formed kingdom. Instead, they sought to establish themselves and confirm the division by having their own centre of worship. They worshipped their own man-made gods. They had "sown the wind" and they would "reap the whirlwind". They sought Gentile ways and associations and "the strangers" would "swallow them up" (v. 7). This is an illustration of something which is made necessary in the purpose of God, because of man's wickedness, rather than one of those eternal truths built into His purpose from the beginning.

By choice Ephraim went up to Assyria to obtain help for which he had to pay, whilst all the time God's help was available and free. As a "wild ass" Ephraim persisted in going his own way. He made altars to sin and the altars would be sin to Him! It is left to Jesus to break in the wild ass and this he prefigured as he journeyed to Jerusalem, riding the colt whereon never man sat.

"THE GREAT THINGS OF MY LAW"
VERSES 12-14

12 I have written to him the great things of my law, but they were counted as a strange thing.

13 They sacrifice flesh for the sacrifices of mine offerings, and eat it; but the LORD accepteth them not; now will he remember their iniquity, and visit their sins: they shall return to Egypt.

14 For Israel hath forgotten his Maker, and buildeth temples; and Judah hath multiplied fenced cities: but I will send a fire upon his cities, and it shall devour the palaces thereof.

The Law of Moses was not just a series of laws, it was a way of life which if kept brought rich blessings. Israel were given the Law, but they became mere custodians of it. They became signposts which pointed the way without themselves moving in the right direction. They offered their sacrifices, but it was without understanding, so that they only "sacrificed flesh". They were involved in the fabric of the Law but in such a way that "the Lord accepteth them not". It is a sobering thought, that in the offering of sacrifices one can actually be guilty of sin. But this is bound to be the case when one's way is set in the direction indicated by verse 14.

Israel had "forgotten" God. The word really implies neglecting. They had become involved in the building of temples and the multiplying of fenced cities, in the setting up of their own forms of worship and the creating of their own defences. How strange that they should exchange "the great things of God's law" for their own self-conceived idolatry and forsake His protection for flimsy self-erected defences. There could only be one end: "I will send a fire upon his cities, and it shall devour the palaces thereof."

9

"REJOICE NOT, O ISRAEL"
VERSES 1-6

*R*EJOICE not, O Israel, for joy, as other people: for thou hast gone a whoring from thy God, thou hast loved a reward upon every cornfloor.

2 The floor and the winepress shall not feed them, and the new wine shall fail in her.

3 They shall not dwell in the LORD's land; but Ephraim shall return to Egypt, and they shall eat unclean things in Assyria.

4 They shall not offer wine offerings to the LORD, neither shall they be pleasing unto him: their sacrifices shall be unto them as the bread of mourners; all that eat thereof shall be polluted: for their bread for their soul shall not come into the house of the LORD.

5 What will ye do in the solemn day, and in the day of the feast of the LORD?

6 For, lo, they are gone because of destruction: Egypt shall gather them up, Memphis shall bury them: the pleasant places for their silver, nettles shall possess them: thorns shall be in their tabernacles.

*R*EJOICING was an integral part of God's way of life. The people had good reason to rejoice, being richly blessed by the God who had delivered them: "Blessed shalt thou be in the city, blessed shalt thou be in the field. Blessed shall be the fruit of thy body, and the fruit of thy ground, and the fruit of thy cattle, the increase of thy kine, and the flocks of thy sheep. Blessed shall be thy basket and thy store. Blessed shalt thou be when thou comest in, and blessed shalt thou be when thou goest out" (Deuteronomy 28:3-6). But the rejoicing was not left to the casual whim of the people: it was built into their new way of life.

God knew how easily man's rejoicing was conditioned by his

human thinking; how man would so often rejoice because of the blessings without pausing to consider that God provided them. Like Gomer, who attributed Hosea's provisions to her lovers, so man rejoices in the good things of God's providing but attributes them to other sources.

So God built rejoicing into their new way of life in such a way that they would appreciate the source of their blessings. At the time of harvest when God's goodness was apparent, they were to mingle together rejoicing with their thankfulness. "And thou shalt rejoice in thy feast, thou and thy son, and thy daughter . . . and the Levite, the stranger, and the fatherless, and the widow, that are within thy gates . . . therefore thou shalt surely rejoice" (Deuteronomy 16:13-15). In the sharing of their blessings with those who were in greater need than themselves, their rejoicing would take on another dimension—it would be a rejoicing based upon their Provider, a principle which they now shared with others.

To be recipients of the blessings of God, however, meant that they also carried greater responsibilities; for it is axiomatic that where there is knowledge there is responsibility (Romans 2:12; 4:15; 5:13). Failure to keep the way of life which brought the blessings led the people into God's judgements. They were not "as other people" any longer. They had been called to be responsible citizens of Zion but they never really renounced their citizenship of Egypt, and so "they would return to Egypt". The promises of God are indeed very great and the price of separation is a very small price to pay for them, but it is a price which must be paid, for lack of separation means loss of the citizenship of Zion.

As God had said: "Therefore will I return, and take away my corn in the time thereof, and my wine in the season thereof" (2:9); so Israel in a strange land would no longer have harvests and would no longer be able to rejoice at the time of ingathering. No longer would they have the necessary things to offer as sacrifices to their God; instead, as the unclean person under the law who was separated from the temple services, so they in a strange land could only eat "the bread of mourners". As a harlot Israel had sought "a reward upon every cornfloor", heedless of the consequences. The

The pleasures she had known were damaging; they were defiling, they were costly, they were not really pleasures at all. They were nothing compared with the wholesome rejoicing of God's way of life. "What will ye do in the solemn day, and in the day of the feast of the LORD?" (v. 5). Egypt would gather them up; Memphis, a royal city of Egypt, would bury them, whilst thorns would be in their tabernacles (v. 6).

"EPHRAIM IS SMITTEN, THEIR ROOT IS DRIED UP"

VERSES 7-17

7 The days of visitation are come, the days of recompence are come; Israel shall know it: the prophet is a fool, the spiritual man is mad, for the multitude of thine iniquity, and the great hatred.

8 The watchman of Ephraim was with my God: but the prophet is a snare of a fowler in all his ways, and hatred in the house of his God.

9 They have deeply corrupted themselves, as in the days of Gibeah: therefore he will remember their iniquity, he will visit their sins.

10 I found Israel like grapes in the wilderness; I saw your fathers as the firstripe in the fig tree at her first time: but they went to Baal-peor, and separated themselves unto that shame; and their abominations were according as they loved.

11 As for Ephraim, their glory shall fly away like a bird, from the birth, and from the womb, and from the conception.

12 Though they bring up their children, yet will I bereave them, that there shall not be a man left: yea, woe also to them when I depart from them!

13 Ephraim, as I saw Tyrus, is planted in a pleasant place: but Ephraim shall bring forth his children to the murderer.

14 Give them, O LORD: what wilt thou give? give them a miscarrying womb and dry breasts.

15 All their wickedness is in Gilgal: for there I hated them: for the wickedness of their doings I will drive them out of mine house, I will love them no more: all their princes are revolters.

16 Ephraim is smitten, their root is dried up, they shall bear no fruit: yea, though they bring forth, yet will I slay even the beloved fruit of their womb.

17 My God will cast them away, because they did not hearken unto him: and they shall be wanderers among the nations.

The people had made their priests like unto themselves (4:9), they had made drunken and murdered their kings (7:5-7) and now we read, "The prophet is a fool, the spiritual man is mad" (9:7). It was all their own doing; "they have deeply corrupted themselves" (v. 9) and so they would reap what they had sown! Of their own choice they had priests and prophets who were corrupted and now became a "snare and a fowler" even "in the house of his God". The watchmen which had originally been for God had now become "a snare on Mizpah, and a net spread upon Tabor" (5:1); note again the play on the names of Mizpah (*watch tower*) and Tabor (*mountain of height*). Their watchmen had become a snare even in the mountain of the Lord.

They had repeated the corruption of Gibeah (also meaning *height*) when the dreadful behaviour of the Benjamites had led to an almost complete annihilation of that tribe (Judges 19 & 20); therefore God would "remember their iniquity" and He would "visit their sins" (v. 9).

Israel had been found "like grapes in the wilderness"; they were as fruit in a barren land, and like the firstfruits which were to be presented to the LORD (v. 10). Unlike Jesus who also was "as a tender plant, and as a root out of a dry ground" (Isaiah 53:2), they never sought their place in the house of the LORD. Instead "they went to Baal-peor, and separated themselves unto that shame".

Note again how they had none to blame but themselves—"They went", "separated themselves", "according as they loved". They chose to follow the counsel of Balaam, who because of his intense greed for money taught Balak to cast a stumblingblock before the Children of Israel. He had encouraged marriage with the alien so that Israel might be first defiled and then destroyed to the benefit of Balak and his own personal gain (see Numbers 25:3-5; 31:16; Revelation 2:14; Jude 11), for God had said Israel shall dwell alone (Numbers 23:9). It was the continual story of Israel: "Their abominations were according as they loved."

The glory of Ephraim (*doubly fruitful*) would depart as a frightened bird; there would be no birth from the womb nor any conception within the womb (v. 11). Should they bring up any children, it would not be to manhood: "Yet will I bereave them, that there shall not be a man left: yea, woe also to them when I depart from them" (v. 12). Left to themselves the nation of Israel would perish. Though once pleasant as Tyrus, now Ephraim would bring forth for the murderer. And she would have "a miscarrying womb and dry breasts" (v. 14).

They had turned Gilgal, the place of blessing where God had rolled away the sins of His people, into a place of wickedness and so there is a dreadful finality about this pronouncement of Ephraim's end: no children; driven out of God's house; loved no more by Him; their root dried up; bearing no fruit; God would cast them away. As a separate nation, the ten tribes were to cease; the remnant which would be saved, would be part of a new kingdom incorporating all the tribes, and a people chosen from amongst the Gentiles.

We cannot close this chapter without reflecting upon a most important principle. Man needs no help to destroy himself! Where God withdraws His protection the end follows speedily. Israel chose for themselves the path they would tread and that path involved denial of the God who had delivered them, up to that point in their lives. Now, since they had left Him and repeatedly refused His offers of help, He would leave them to destroy themselves. To choose any pathway which involves walking in our own strength is suicidal, since, "the way of man is not in himself: it is not in man that walketh to direct his steps" (Jeremiah 10:23).

10

"THEIR HEART IS DIVIDED"
VERSES 1-9

*I*SRAEL *is an empty vine, he bringeth forth fruit unto himself: according to the multitude of his fruit he hath increased the altars; according to the goodness of his land they have made goodly images.*

2 Their heart is divided; now shall they be found faulty: he shall break down their altars, he shall spoil their images.

3 For now they shall say, We have no king, because we feared not the LORD; what then should a king do to us?

4 They have spoken words, swearing falsely in making a covenant: thus judgment springeth up as hemlock in the furrows of the field.

5 The inhabitants of Samaria shall fear because of the calves of Beth-aven: for the people thereof shall mourn over it, and the priests thereof that rejoiced on it, for the glory thereof, because it is departed from it.

6 It shall be also carried unto Assyria for a present to king Jareb: Ephraim shall receive shame, and Israel shall be ashamed of his own counsel.

7 As for Samaria, her king is cut off as the foam upon the water.

8 The high places also of Aven, the sin of Israel, shall be destroyed: the thorn and the thistle shall come up on their altars; and they shall say to the mountains, Cover us; and to the hills, Fall on us.

9 O Israel, thou hast sinned from the days of Gibeah: there they stood: the battle in Gibeah against the children of iniquity did not overtake them.

THIS chapter begins by presenting a problem: "Israel is an empty vine, he bringeth forth fruit unto himself." How can a vine be at the same time both empty and fruitful? Some have said

66

the translation should be "luxuriant vine", meaning that the vine was rich in leafy growth but lacking in fruit. It is a well-known fact that fruiting trees can spend their strength upon leafy growth and have little left for the bearing of fruit, and this interpretation is not without sound exhortational value. Israel had spent their strength on a selfish display of glory which had no fruit for God who had so richly blessed them. The context, however, would suggest that the vine had been exceedingly fruitful, but that the fruit had been grossly misused. The vine had brought forth a "multitude" of fruit but it had been wasted upon their idolatry.

The chapter begins therefore by picking up a point made in chapter 2 and then enlarging upon it: "For she did not know that I gave her corn, and wine, and oil, and multiplied her silver and gold, which they prepared for Baal." They greedily devoured the gifts but they were unconscious of the giver. As the blessings increased, so did their idolatry.

It is the prophet Ezekiel who explains that a vine has no other purpose than to bear fruit. It is of no value as timber and when it does not yield fruit, unlike other trees of the forest, it is good only as fuel for the fire (Ezekiel 15). There is very good reason then why the vine is used not only as a symbol of Israel but also of Jesus and his disciples (John 15). What we have and are is all of God, and it is fatal to devote to self-gratification what He has given to us; to spend God-given blessings on godless pursuits!

The reason this happened in Israel is because "their heart is divided" (v. 2). Did not the prophet Elijah reprimand them, saying, "How long halt ye between two opinions?" And does not the apostle James add to this counsel by saying, "A double minded man is unstable in all his ways" (1:8)? The danger of this sin is that it does not involve an outright rejection of God. Whilst following his own course man still regards himself as being faithful to God. Fundamentally man is foolish enough to think that he can have the best of both worlds; momentarily he forgets that he cannot serve God and mammon. He who is joined to an idol is one with that idol and since God cannot be associated with an idol, union with Him must then end.

Seeking "lovers" had been all Israel's own doing, but now God would act: "He shall break down their altars, he shall spoil their images" (v. 2). But even worse for them, the time would come when they would be without a king (v. 3). The divided heart would lead them to the loss of both true and false rulers. As chapter 3 made so clear, the time would come when they would be without king, without sacrifice, without image and without ephod. To set the heart on the kingdom of God and His righteousness is to be blessed by His goodness now and in His kingdom later; but to be divided in loyalties is to lose all!

There is more than a hint of Israel's final overthrow prior to the establishment of God's kingdom in verse 4, where in speaking of their false covenant God says: "Thus judgment springeth up as hemlock in the furrows of the field." The first application is of course of God's judgements on the fruits of their daily lives bringing about utter and complete desolation. But it must also be noted that the original word for hemlock is *rosh*, which takes us into Ezekiel 38 where we see the final invasion of the land when the chief prince of *Rosh* will go to take a spoil. This is not an isolated reference in this chapter to the time of the end, as we shall see, and as we have already noticed there are frequent references made to the kingdom of God throughout this prophecy.

Their glory—which had been centred in calf worship introduced by Jeroboam, who had hoped by this step to prevent a healing of the breach between the ten and the two tribes (1 Kings 12)—was departed and Hosea in irony speaks of "Beth-aven"—*House of wickedness*, instead of "Beth-el"—*House of God* (v. 5). King Jareb, whose help Israel sought (5:13), instead of helping, devoured Israel's glory (v. 6). Truly, the strangers amongst which Israel mixed devoured her strength (7:8). Now she would know it!

The wording of verse 7 is uncertain, but the meaning is clear. Their king would be cut off, either as transient foam which soon disappears, or (R.V.) as overhanging twigs which are cut off at the water's surface. This is referred to again in the last verse of this chapter where "Beth-el" is seen to triumph over "Beth-aven" and Hoshea their last king is "utterly cut off".

Their high places of "Aven" (*wickedness*) would be destroyed, and the curse of "thorns and thistles" which resulted from Adam's transgression would burst forth from their altars. Although these words were fulfilled in the overthrowing of the kingdom, Jesus applies the latter part of this verse to God's final judgement upon His people: "And they shall say to the mountains, Cover us; and to the hills, Fall on us" (v. 8). Not cured by the severe punishment following the transgression at Gibeah, further punishment would follow (v. 9).

"SOW IN RIGHTEOUSNESS AND REAP IN MERCY"
VERSES 10-15

10 It is in my desire that I should chastise them; and the people shall be gathered against them, when they shall bind themselves in their two furrows.

11 And Ephraim is as an heifer that is taught, and loveth to tread out the corn; but I passed over upon her fair neck: I will make Ephraim to ride; Judah shall plow, and Jacob shall break his clods.

12 Sow to yourselves in righteousness, reap in mercy; break up your fallow ground: for it is time to seek the LORD, till he come and rain righteousness upon you.

13 Ye have plowed wickedness, ye have reaped iniquity; ye have eaten the fruit of lies: because thou didst trust in thy way, in the multitude of thy mighty men.

14 Therefore shall a tumult arise among thy people, and all thy fortresses shall be spoiled, as Shalman spoiled Beth-arbel in the day of battle: the mother was dashed in pieces upon her children.

15 So shall Beth-el do unto you because of your great wickedness: in a morning shall the king of Israel utterly be cut off.

Looking back through the writings of Hosea, we are able to see that Israel did not repent and therefore the hand of God was heavy upon them. We are also able to see that God's judgements will fall yet again upon their descendants, but this additional knowledge which we are given must not obscure the great lesson which runs throughout this book: that His afflictions were remedial. God was giving His people, though undeserving, the opportunity to repent and thus avoid the final desolation.

There is, therefore, an unusual mixture of exhortation and final judgement running side by side throughout this prophecy; exhortation to lead the people to righteousness and yet, because of the foreknowledge of God by which He knew they would not heed His call, the warning of what really lay ahead. It is because man is given a free will that God also gives to him every opportunity to do the right thing; He does not allow His own foreknowledge of a situation to short-circuit the events. In this way a seed will ultimately be born which will be redeemed and which will survive the final judgements upon the world. A good illustration of this principle is seen in the fact that although God knew that Nineveh would become so wicked that He would ultimately say to her, "There is no healing of thy bruise" (Nahum 3:19), this did not prevent Him from sending Jonah to them with an opportunity for penitence. It is this calling which opens up great possibilities for us, for as the apostle Peter wrote, "God is long suffering to us-ward, not willing that any should perish" (2 Peter 3:9). That call has gone forth and along with it the warning of what is to be faced by any who should wilfully turn aside.

The remedial nature of God's actions is seen in the use of the two words "desire" and "chastise" (v. 10), which express God's "longing" to "instruct" the people. They have failed to respond to all previous exhortations and so God will gather together the nations as the Israelites were gathered together against the tribe of Benjamin after their transgression at Gibeah. The exact meaning of "their two furrows" is uncertain as the word only occurs here and in Exodus where it is translated "duty of marriage". Probably the prophet was making reference to the way in which they were bound, as in marriage, to the idolatrous worship of their two calves, in the sense in which Paul says, "He which is joined to a harlot is one body" with that harlot. The nations to which Ephraim had yoked herself would now "ride" her; she would know the burden which would be placed upon her as along with the royal tribe she ploughed and broke up the clods of earth: "Ye have plowed wickedness, ye have reaped iniquity; ye have eaten the fruit of lies: because thou didst trust in thy way, in the multitude of thy mighty men. Therefore shall a tumult arise among thy people and all thy fortresses shall be spoiled."

This simple, basic, though hard, labour leads naturally to the exhortation of verse 12, an exhortation which is good for all time and for all people: "Sow to yourselves." Salvation is an individual matter and each must ensure that he is sowing "in righteousness". Righteousness does not refer to perfection of character, but to the way of life we should be following. It is not living a flawless life but rather is it *following* a flawless way of life. It is believing and accepting the principles of God's way of life in such a way that even though we fail through weakness to honour His high standards, by adherence to His principles of salvation we can still be approved in His sight. "Reap in mercy" is not a deserved harvest, since none can earn or merit in any way the mercy of God. It is a promised blessing consequent upon the acceptance of God's way of life; it represents God's response to those who seek to honour His name and who, even though human weakness will be revealed in their lives from time to time, can never be guilty of wilful rebellion against the One whom they have covenanted to serve. Rebellion is the product of "double mindedness" and can never be entertained by those following Paul's counsel: "Let this mind be in you, which was also in Christ Jesus" (Philippians 2:5).

"Break up your fallow ground." Hard trampled ground will not receive the refreshing rain when it comes, nor will a hardened heart be the place for the mercy of God. Furthermore, the work of breaking up the ground must be done before the rains start, so the prophet goes on to say: "For it is time to seek the Lord, till he come and rain righteousness upon you." Breaking up the fallow ground is constructive, it is creative, it is preparatory to the sowing *and* the

71

harvest; it is also essential since seed falling upon hard ground will not bear fruit!

"Till he come." This must be a dominating thought and a motivating principle. It must be a living hope. For the Christian believer it must be the belief which guides all his decisions. Jesus is coming back, and until he comes there can be no real satisfaction in this life (see comments on 6:3).

"And rain righteousness upon you." This is a different word from the "righteousness" used earlier in this verse and refers to something new. The righteousness which Jesus will bring with him and which he will bestow upon the faithful will be a share in God's righteousness. Jeremiah says, "He shall be called, THE LORD OUR RIGHTEOUSNESS" (23:6) and he adds a little later: "In those days shall Judah be saved, and Jerusalem shall dwell safely: and this is the name wherewith she shall be called, The LORD our righteousness" (33:16). The new "bride" will be presented faultless before the presence of His glory (Jude 24): this is the blessing for those who sow in righteousness and break up their fallow ground. He will come and rain righteousness upon them.

The prophet Isaiah adds to this figure: "For as the rain cometh down, and the snow from heaven, and returneth not thither, but watereth the earth, and maketh it bring forth and bud, that it may give seed to the sower, and bread to the eater: so shall my word be that goeth forth out of my mouth: it shall not return unto me void, but it shall accomplish that which I please, and it shall prosper in the thing whereto I sent it" (Isaiah 55:10,11). The rains from heaven cause the seed to provide a harvest from which the farmer may have bread to eat and seed to sow for the next harvest. So the word of God provides the food we need and the seed which we must sow. In this way God will accomplish His purpose: "For ye shall go out with joy, and be led forth with peace: the mountains and the hills shall break forth before you into singing, and all the trees of the field shall clap their hands." Working with and feeding upon the word of God is the only way to that final harvest when He will "come and rain righteousness upon you".

72

Israel had ploughed wickedness and reaped iniquity. They had eaten the fruit of their own lies and trusted in their own mighty men (v. 13). What a contrast to sowing in righteousness and reaping in mercy! "Beth-arbel", *the House of God's court*, would be spoiled by Shalmaneser (v. 14), but "Beth-el", *the House of God*, would triumph over their wickedness and there would be a great mourning. In 721 B.C. Hoshea, their last king, was taken captive and their nation spoiled (2 Kings 17:1-6). What happened to Israel then was only a partial fulfilment of this prophecy, as is evident from this chapter. The repeated wickedness of Israel throughout their generations will result in a final overthrow of their pride and self confidence, prior to the return of Jesus who will then establish the long promised Kingdom.

11

"WHEN ISRAEL WAS A CHILD, THEN I LOVED HIM"

VERSES 1-4

*W*HEN *Israel was a child, then I loved him, and called my son out of Egypt.*

2 As they called them, so they went from them: they sacrificed unto Baalim, and burned incense to graven images.

3 I taught Ephraim also to go, taking them by their arms; but they knew not that I healed them.

4 I drew them with cords of a man, with bands of love: and I was to them as they that take off the yoke on their jaws, and I laid meat unto them.

THERE is a very graphic picture of Israel's calling recorded in Ezekiel 16 which nothing but the unqualified love of God could possibly have accomplished. An unwashed, unclean, unpitied, unswaddled child, polluted in its own blood and left to die, is taken by God and brought up to be an exceedingly beautiful woman, expensively dressed and ornamented. There was nothing about the child to call forth such love and care, and that which it represents of Israel's calling can only be explained by God's words: "The Lord did not set his love upon you, nor choose you, because ye were more in number than any people; for ye were the fewest of all people: but because the Lord loved you" (Deuteronomy 7:7,8).

Perhaps it is in the Epistles of John that we learn most about this unique quality of love which is so unlike any human emotion. He teaches us that whilst man may be lovely, God is love! Love is inseparable from the nature and character of God (1 John 4:8).

74

Because of this He makes sacrifice with purpose (1 John 3:16); He makes undeserved propitiation for our sins (1 John 4:10), and seeks to make us His sons and daughters (1 John 3:1). There is no reason why any of these things should be done; it is just that God is love! So it was that God loved Israel "and called His son out of Egypt".

These words are of course prophetic, since whilst it is true that the nation of Israel was called out of Egypt, enshrined in that calling was the more important calling of God's only begotten Son. Had Israel become extinct following their slavery in Egypt, the royal line would have ceased; no child could have been born through Mary who would himself be called forth out of Egypt at a later time in their history. And so whilst God did love Israel and deliver them from slavery, His real expression of love is for His beloved Son in whom He was well pleased, the one who would himself appreciate the real meaning of "my son" and the one without whom the whole history of Israel would be pointless.

The response of His Son was to be so different from that of Israel for: "The more I called Israel, the further they went from me" (v. 2, N.I.V.). The work of calling was entrusted to faithful prophets (see 12:13), who were ignored and ridiculed. In so doing God was blasphemed, for "they sacrificed unto Baalim, and burned incense to graven images".

The next two verses use the tender imagery of a father's care for his child as he teaches it to walk and provides the necessary food. Yet as a young child is selfish in its demands for help and food, not realising all the care which is provided, so of Israel God says, "But they knew not that I healed them".

There is another indication of the continuing fulfilment of God's predictions in verse 4: "I drew them with cords of a man, with bands of love." The figure is of course that of a father teaching his child to walk as he guides and supports him in cords or reins, but the expression takes us much further into the history of Israel, where God reaches the climax of His expression of love for His people in seeking to draw them, and all men, unto Himself by the "cords of a man". The man is Jesus Christ, who expressly stated,

75

"No man can come to me, except the Father which hath sent me draw him" (John 6:44). In him alone can mankind come to the Father and in him is God's greatest expression of love: "For God so loved the world, that he gave his only begotten Son, that whosoever believeth in him should not perish, but have everlasting life." By him God "laid meat unto them" by giving him as the "bread of life".

"MY PEOPLE ARE BENT TO BACKSLIDING"
VERSES 5-7

5 He shall not return into the land of Egypt, but the Assyrian shall be his king, because they refused to return.

6 And the sword shall abide on his cities, and shall consume his branches, and devour them, because of their own counsels.

7 And my people are bent to backsliding from me: though they called them to the most High, none at all would exalt him.

The prophets "called them to the most High" but the people refused to "exalt him". Jeremiah describes how God sought to guide His people along the right path, "rising early" to do so. Jeremiah makes use of this expression eleven times and on each occasion he uses it to describe God's anxious care for a wayward people. It is a figure of speech based upon the early rising of the servant who saddles the mules in readiness for the day's journey and depicts God rising early to prevent His people from committing iniquity as they rise early, only to tarry with strong drink until even!

Despite the loving care lavished upon Israel, she did not turn to God when faced by the Assyrians but instead sought help from Egypt. Thus God says, "He shall not return to the land of Egypt, but the Assyrian shall be his king". How typical of human nature which turns so freely for help to the life which should have been completely abandoned, which despite having been "called out of Egypt" chooses instead to return to its slavery.

The long history of Israel shows that even though God had toiled with them over many years they would still choose to return to Egypt from where they had been delivered. Future generations, too, would place their confidence in other than the true God, only to find God's words to their fathers applicable also to themselves: "And the sword shall abide on his cities, and shall consume his branches, and devour them, because of their own counsels."

"FOR I AM GOD, AND NOT MAN"
VERSES 8-12

8 How shall I give thee up, Ephraim? how shall I deliver thee, Israel? how shall I make thee as Admah? how shall I set thee as Zeboim? mine heart is turned within me, my repentings are kindled together.
9 I will not execute the fierceness of mine anger, I will not return to destroy Ephraim: for I am God, and not man; the Holy One in the midst of thee: and I will not enter into the city.
10 They shall walk after the LORD: he shall roar like a lion: when he shall roar, then the children shall tremble from the west.
11 They shall tremble as a bird out of Egypt, and as a dove out of the land of Assyria: and I will place them in their houses, saith the LORD.
12 Ephraim compasseth me about with lies, and the house of Israel with deceit: but Judah yet ruleth with God, and is faithful with the saints.

There is an intensity of emotion released in the words, "How shall I give thee up, Ephraim? . . . mine heart is turned within me, my repentings are kindled together", and although we cannot attribute human emotion to God, we cannot dispose of this verse by just saying that God is speaking in a way that we can understand, or that He is speaking in the idiom of Hosea's experiences with Gomer, although that is of course true. We are in fact looking at God's deep concern for Israel and in so doing are being given an insight into the depth of feeling and love which is behind the Atonement. Thus the Old Testament prepares us for great declarations in the New, such as "God so loved the world", and "Whilst we were yet sinners, Christ died for us"—verses which reveal more clearly just how God will complete His purpose. Jeremiah captures this same picture relative to Israel: "Is Ephraim my dear son? is he a pleasant child? for since I spake against him, I do earnestly remember him still: therefore my bowels are troubled for him; I will surely have mercy upon him, saith the LORD" (31:20).

Though we can explain the Atonement in Scriptural terms and understand the justice and logic of it, we shall never understand the heart of God in His conception and execution of it. Like the apostles, we are left searching for adequate words to describe it— "exceeding great and precious promises", "the riches of his grace", "exceeding riches of his grace in his kindness toward us through Christ", "the unsearchable riches of Christ", "exceeding abundantly above all that we ask or think" to mention just a few of the occasions where New Testament writers seem to be at a loss to express in human terms the heart behind the Atonement.

Despite the backsliding of Israel, there is still work to be done. She cannot be obliterated like the cities of the plain, "Admah and Zeboim". "I will not return to destroy Ephraim: for I am God, and not man." Just as there is no explanation for the love of God other than that God is love, so the only explanation of God's response to sin is that He is God and not man! Man seeks his vengeance to the full; God conceives remedial chastisement. He will not make a full end of Israel as He had of the cities of the plain. There will be chastisement, but it will not be executed "in the fierceness" of His anger; He will "not return to destroy Ephraim"; a seed will be preserved to sing the words of Isaiah: "And in that day thou shalt say, O LORD, I will praise thee: though thou wast angry with me, thine anger is turned away, and thou comfortedst me. Behold, God is my salvation . . . Cry out and shout, thou inhabitant of Zion: for great is the Holy One in the midst of thee'' (12:1,2,6).

That generation will perish in its iniquity but a people will live to know of ''the Holy One'' in their midst, when ''He shall roar as a lion''. Their descentants will then ''tremble as a bird'' as they are brought back into the land from Egypt and Assyria, from the east and from the west (Zechariah 8:7). Speaking of this day the prophet Joel says: ''The LORD also shall roar out of Zion, and utter His voice from Jerusalem; and the heavens and the earth shall shake: but the LORD will be the hope of his people, and the strength of the children of Israel. So shall ye know that I am the LORD your God dwelling in Zion'' (3:16,17).

12

"THERE GOD SPAKE WITH US"
VERSES 1-4

E PHRAIM *feedeth on wind, and followeth after the east wind: he daily increaseth lies and desolation; and they do make a covenant with the Assyrians, and oil is carried into Egypt.*

2 The LORD hath also a controversy with Judah, and will punish Jacob according to his ways; according to his doings will he recompense him.

3 He took his brother by the heel in the womb, and by his strength he had power with God:

4 Yea, he had power over the angel, and prevailed: he wept, and made supplication unto him: he found him in Beth-el, and there he spake with us;

A JEWISH translation of the Old Testament based on the Masoretic text places the last verse of chapter 11 at the beginning of chapter 12 and this would seem to be the right place for it, since it belongs to the theme of chapter 12. There we see Judah included in the Lord's "controversy" which was first raised with Israel (4:1) and it is under the figure of Jacob's calling that the prophet now speaks. We are reminded of the incidents at Beth-el, where Jacob became acquainted with "the house of God" and received the covenant promises, and where at a later stage, after an angel had wrestled with him, his name was changed from Jacob to Israel. That change of name indicated a development of character; by nature he was "a supplanter", a man of guile or deceit, but by aspiration he was a man of God, or, as his new name indicated, *a prince with God.*

Ephraim had not developed. The people were still "compassed about with lies"; their house was not "Beth-el", it was the house of deceit! They clung to the things the name Jacob stands for and "daily increased lies and desolation". They did not aspire to become "Israel" along with their father, instead they took upon themselves the likeness of the nations amongst whom they mixed: they were "merchants" (Canaanites) with balances of deceit (v. 7).

We read of Jacob that "there wrestled a man with him" (Genesis 32:24); an expression at first symbolising God's continual wrestling with Jacob, but also beyond that to God's wrestlings with His children through "*the* man", the man of God's right hand, the Son of man whom God made strong for Himself. Jacob responded to God's correction but Ephraim did not. Whilst supposed to be in covenant relationship with God, Ephraim was in fact making a "covenant with the Assyrians" and the God-given blessings were being given away to Egypt in payment for the hope of deliverance ("oil is carried into Egypt"), a deliverance which God would have freely wrought on their behalf had they sought His help.

Jacob had "wept and made supplication" unto God. He had recognised his own weakness before his enemies and, like Jesus who many years later would cry unto God with "strong crying and tears", had known that in God was salvation from death. So Jacob, now without guile, had cast himself completely upon his God. Two remarkable statements arose from this humility: "He found him in Beth-el, and there he spake with us" (v. 4). God *found* Jacob in Beth-el: Jacob was lost and God found him. By the deceit practised upon his father and brother, he was isolated from home. He would never see his mother again and many long years would pass before he would see his father, and even then there would be the constant fear of his brother's reprisals. But God found him. God knew the qualities of his character, and how he would respond to chastisement, so when Jacob sought Him in tears, God was quick to answer. There was something special about that answer—"There he spake *with us.*"

Writing of the prophets, Peter has these words: "Unto whom it was revealed, that not unto themselves, but *unto us* they did minister the things, which are now reported unto you" (1 Peter 1:12). The Word of God is a living Word and it has a message for each generation. Although given at a specific time and under specific circumstances its scope is not limited, so what God had to say to Jacob was also good for the people of Hosea's day and by the same principle it is still good for ours. In fact the most important application of the Word, is to that generation which is currently reading it. Hence Hosea says, "There God spake *with us*; even the LORD God of hosts; the LORD is his memorial".

"THE LORD IS HIS MEMORIAL"

VERSES 5,6

5 Even the LORD God of hosts; the LORD is his memorial.
6 Therefore turn thou to thy God: keep mercy and judgment, and wait on thy God continually.

It is because God is speaking to all who will listen that it is essential that each knows who is speaking and what is His authority, hence the reference to the "memorial" name. Firstly we must believe that He is the LORD God of "hosts", that is, of all peoples, nations, angels and all created things (Genesis 2:1; Deuteronomy 4:19; Psalm 33:6 etc.). He is the creator and ruler over all things. He is supreme; but not in any despotic sense. He is a God with purpose; creative and constructive. These latter characteristics are all contained in the Memorial name which speaks of God's salvation in a most remarkable way.

Although the Memorial name, which is always represented in capital letters in the Authorised Version, does occur in the book of Genesis, it is not until we come to Exodus 3 that we read of it as being the name by which God chose to be known both to Moses and to the children of Israel. There we read of the Israelites in deep distress, slaves in Egypt; they were without a leader, their backs bleeding and bent beneath the lash as they toiled daily. It is the reality of that for which the unswaddled child was only the figure and it is in these circumstances that God says, "I have surely seen the affliction of my people which are in Egypt, and have heard their cry by reason of their taskmasters; for I know their sorrows; and I am come down to deliver them" (Exodus 3:7,8). There is certainty in the words: I have seen, I have heard and I have come down! That certainty is embodied in the name by which God is to be introduced to Israel: "I AM THAT I AM", or "I WILL BE THAT I WILL BE".

The name expresses the self-existence of God, the certainty of His being, the unchangeableness of His nature and the complete dependability of His purpose. It is a name which carries these qualities throughout all generations and in some senses it is captured in such descriptions of God as, "I am the Alpha and the Omega", "the same yesterday, and today, and for ever", and its meaning is behind the declaration of Job: "For I know that my redeemer liveth, and that he shall stand at the latter day upon the earth" (19:25). God is a redeemer who ever liveth. It is a name which at one and the same time describes God as a deliverer, and the promise of deliverance itself. It is a name which describes God as the One who reaches out to save His people throughout all ages and therefore it points particularly to Jesus, the one chosen by God to be His representative amongst men and to be the means by which He would offer salvation to all men. It is a name which speaks of the time when God will be "all and in all", when the redeemed will be partakers of His nature and all hearts will beat at the impulse of His will—I WILL BE THAT I WILL BE.

We are not surprised therefore when, after saying that this was the God who was speaking to Israel, Hosea counsels them: "Turn thou to thy God: keep mercy and judgment, and wait on thy God continually"; turn to God and practise His mercy and judgement and continually await His good pleasure. The reader will of course remember that it was not for themselves that the prophets spoke, but that God was speaking *to us*.

"EPHRAIM PROVOKED HIM TO ANGER"

VERSES 7-14

7 He is a merchant, the balances of deceit are in his hand: he loveth to oppress.

8 And Ephraim said, Yet I am become rich, I have found me out substance: in all my labours they shall find none iniquity in me that were sin.

9 And I that am the LORD thy God from the land of Egypt will yet make thee to dwell in tabernacles, as in the days of the solemn feast.

10 I have also spoken by the prophets, and I have multiplied visions, and used similitudes, by the ministry of the prophets.

11 Is there iniquity in Gilead? surely they are vanity: they sacrifice bullocks in Gilgal; yea, their altars are as heaps in the furrows of the fields.

12 And Jacob fled into the country of Syria, and Israel served for a wife, and for a wife he kept sheep.

13 And by a prophet the LORD brought Israel out of Egypt, and by a prophet was he preserved.

14 Ephraim provoked him to anger most bitterly: therefore shall he leave his blood upon him, and his reproach shall his Lord return unto him.

Ephraim could not be further away from the glory of God, which in the Gospel of John is described as "grace and truth" and here in verse 6 as "mercy and judgment". Instead she is a merchant of deceit and loves to oppress. On the one hand, we have the essentials of salvation, the grace of God without which there could be no hope, and His truth which characterises the new way of life to which we are called. On the other, we have the selfish oppression and deceit of man by which he not only abuses others but also destroys himself. The real tragedy is that the deceit which is practised against others also prevents man from recognising the weakness of his own way of life and so Ephraim boasted that her ways had made her rich.

It is so easy to justify behaviour by regarding apparent success as a blessing from God. Conversely, Job's friends regarded Job's poverty and suffering as an indication that he had sinned before God and their all too easy solution was simply to confess the hidden sins. We know from the narrative how wrong they were, but the same deceit in our nature very often prevents us from recognising the truth about ourselves.

There is a principle which is established very early in the Scriptures and which God frequently uses. To Eve God said, "He shall rule over thee." Because she had refused to accept God's order of responsibility voluntarily, God enforced the rule and she was then left without option. Despite modern claims of equality, man has only created an illusion and the fact remains that "he shall rule over thee". The principle, then, is that where God has laid down an important rule and man has refused voluntarily to accept it, that rule is enforced in such a way that he has no further option. Israel refused to accept Jesus when he first came but the time will come when with mourning and tears they will do so.

In verse 9 we see this same principle applied. God says, "I that am the LORD thy God from the land of Egypt will yet make thee to dwell in tabernacles". Ephraim had refused to keep the Law and to observe the solemn feasts but the time is coming when they will keep God's law, and it will be a schoolmaster to bring them unto Christ. Ezekiel writes of the keeping of all the sacrifices and special feast days in God's kingdom and Zechariah describes the punishments which will be inflicted upon any who still persist in going their own way (14:16-21).

These things had been made very clear to Israel through the prophets by whom God had spoken, and verse 10 is one of many which teach that "holy men of God spake as they were moved by the Holy Spirit". Unhappily, the people had not listened: instead they had turned Gilead (the city of balm) into iniquity, and in Gilgal, the place where they had kept their first Passover and their iniquity had been rolled away from them, they were offering strange sacrifices (v. 11).

Once more behind the text we are able to see Hosea's own experiences. In verse 12 God reminds the people how Jacob had sought and by his labour had purchased a wife (just as Hosea had sought out and later purchased Gomer), and by this illustration Israel is reminded how God had brought them out of Egypt. The figures are intended to remind Israel of the very special care and attention given to them, and thus emphasise the evil of their rejection of Him and consequently the justice of God's rejection of them (v. 14).

13

"WHEN HE OFFENDED IN BAAL, HE DIED"
VERSES 1-8

*W*HEN *Ephraim spake trembling, he exalted himself in Israel; but when he offended in Baal, he died.*

2 And now they sin more and more, and have made them molten images of their silver, and idols according to their own understanding, all of it the work of the craftsmen: they say of them, Let the men that sacrifice kiss the calves.

3 Therefore they shall be as the morning cloud, and as the early dew that passeth away, as the chaff that is driven with the whirlwind out of the floor, and as the smoke out of the chimney.

4 Yet I am the LORD *thy God from the land of Egypt, and thou shalt know no god but me: for there is no saviour beside me.*

5 I did know thee in the wilderness, in the land of great drought.

6 According to their pasture, so were they filled; they were filled, and their heart was exalted; therefore have they forgotten me.

7 Therefore I will be unto them as a lion: as a leopard by the way will I observe them:

8 I will meet them as a bear that is bereaved of her whelps, and will rend the caul of their heart, and there will I devour them like a lion: the wild beast shall tear them.

ONCE more we have running, side by side, the complete desolation of the ten tribe kingdom perishing in its iniquity, and the longer view in which the kingdom of God is established and His purpose with the twelve tribes fulfilled. The chapter opens, "When Ephraim spake trembling, he exalted himself". Since there was no time in the history of the ten tribe kingdom when they humbled themselves before God, the Revised Version seems to be more correct: "When Ephraim spake, there was trembling." It is a statement of what Ephraim was and the power which she had initially; but unhappily the verse concludes: "But when he offended in Baal, he died."

From the very beginning of the kingdom the people were involved in idolatry, their course was set and they died. No attempt was made to redeem the situation, but instead each successive king led the people further into heathen ways. We have already seen the people condemned as being without knowledge: here Hosea upbraids them for using craftsmen to turn their silver into idols in accordance with "their own understanding".

How strange that they should reject a complete and successful system of worship in favour of their self-manufactured religion; and turn their backs upon God, the source of their strength and riches, to worship instead idols which their craftsmen had made in accordance with their instructions. How deceitful is the heart of man which clouds his vision and leads him into the acceptance of those things which destroy; to reject life in favour of death; and above all, into thinking that we, personally, are immune!

The transience of their way of life is emphasised by three examples:

as the *early dew* they will pass away;

as the *chaff* they will be driven away by the wind, and

as *smoke* from a chimney they would disappear.

It is only when fortified by the wisdom of God's Word that man is able to see things as they really are, to know that those things which take over our lives are but the chaff of the summer threshing floor. It was by this faith that Moses could see God's people in the slaves in Egypt, and to recognise in all the splendour of Egypt the transience of sin. There can be no substitute for daily sustenance from God's Word and the humility to follow where it leads. Without these things lesser thoughts will claim an undue proportion of our lives and things which have no lasting value will take the central place.

Israel had known God from their birth, they had seen His strength and known of His willingness to deliver. Now without Him they would know that there is no other god with the power to save (v. 4).

Anything that claims to be a god must have the power to save. The LORD Himself makes this point very clear through Isaiah in a series of statements recorded in chapter 45:

Israel shall be saved in the LORD (v. 17);

Graven images cannot save (v. 20);

There is no God else beside me, a just god and a Saviour (v. 21);

Because of these qualities every knee shall bow to Him (v. 23).

The apostle Paul picks up this theme and shows how God completes this promise in His Son (whose name, exalted above every name, means *saviour*), to whom every knee will bow, to the glory of God (Philippians 2:1-11).

When applied to our life this simple test shows the worthlessness of the many gods which still are worshipped, though of course none of the worshippers think themselves to be guilty of putting their trust in anything but God. The reason for this is explained in verses 5 and 6, where we read that although God had supplied all their needs, even under wilderness conditions, the people had become exalted in their affluence—accepting the provisions but forgetting the Provider! The remedy, as seen in chapter 2, had to be in the removal of His blessings, but since Israel still did not turn to God there could be only one final answer. The nation must be destroyed. So under the figure of being torn by wild beasts (v. 8), God foretells their overthrow by the surrounding nations.

"I WILL BE THY KING"

VERSES 9-16

9 O Israel, thou hast destroyed thyself; but in me is thine help.

10 I will be thy king: where is any other that may save thee in all thy cities? and thy judges of whom thou saidst, Give me a king and princes?

11 I gave thee a king in mine anger, and took him away in my wrath.

12 The iniquity of Ephraim is bound up; his sin is hid.

13 The sorrows of a travailing woman shall come upon him: he is an unwise son; for he should not stay long in the place of the breaking forth of children.

14 I will ransom them from the power of the grave; I will redeem them from death: O death, I will be thy plagues; O grave, I will be thy destruction: repentance shall be hid from mine eyes.

15 Though he be fruitful among his brethren, an east wind shall come, the wind of the LORD shall come up from the wilderness, and his spring shall become dry, and his fountain shall be dried up: he shall spoil the treasure of all pleasant vessels.

16 Samaria shall become desolate; for she hath rebelled against her God: they shall fall by the sword: their infants shall be dashed in pieces, and their women with child shall be ripped up.

Whilst it was true that God foretold the destruction of Israel, verse 9 makes it quite clear that that destruction was all Israel's own doing: "O Israel, thou hast destroyed thyself." Isaiah makes the same point; speaking of Israel's broken marriage he says: "Thus saith the LORD, Where is the bill of your mother's divorcement, whom I have put away? or which of my creditors is it to whom I have sold you? Behold, for your iniquities have ye sold yourselves, and for your transgressions is your mother put away" (50:1). In other words, there *is* a divorce, you *have* been sold, but the responsibility is entirely with you. Again in Isaiah we read: "But your iniquities have separated between you and your God, and your sins have hid his face from you, that he will not hear" (59:2). God is seen to confirm what man has already accomplished and a withdrawal of His protection permits man's destruction to take place. How tragic for Israel when help was so near—"but in me is thine help".

"The iniquity of Ephraim is bound up; his sin is hid" (v. 12). Like David who had sought to hide his sin but who had been given no rest until he confessed it (Psalm 32), so Ephraim was to be chastised with the hope of a confession which would bring deliverance. The chastisement is seen in the figure of a woman in travail, whose pains herald the birth of a child which if not delivered will bring the death of it and the mother. In Ephraim the chastisement does not lead to birth: "He is an unwise son; for he should not stay long in the place of breaking forth of children" (v. 13). The tragedy of travail without a subsequent birth is something which only those who have experienced it will understand to the full. Many months of waiting, hours of pain endured in anticipation—but all to no avail. This was Ephraim's position but she was so corrupted by pleasure that she did not appreciate it.

The "fruitfulness" of Ephraim, though seen by his brethren, would be consumed by an east wind (v. 15). The invasion would come from Assyria and there would be no mercy. The dreadful things foretold in verse 16 were fulfilled to Israel's horror and at a time when it was too late to repent.

Samaria became desolate and the ten tribe kingdom was no more, but the purpose of God was not frustrated. He will accomplish that which He has declared: He will be that He will be! So we read in verse 14, a verse from which the apostle Paul quotes (1 Corinthians 15:55), thus leaving us in no doubt of its future fulfilment: "I will ransom them from the power of the grave; I will redeem them from death: O death, I will be thy plagues; O grave, I will be thy destruction: repentance shall be hid from mine eyes."

Paul confirms our previous conclusions by his use of this verse.

God's purpose will not be fulfilled in a re-established ten-tribe kingdom, but in a kingdom which will be comprised of people out of all tribes and all nations. They will all have one thing in common; humbly they will have confessed their unworthiness and will have accepted God's salvation in Jesus. Even death will be no barrier, for God will buy them back from the grave and redeem them from death. This is a much greater thing than just the re-establishment of the twelve tribes, though that of course will occur; this will be the merchant selling all his goodly pearls to buy the one "pearl of great price". It will be the time when Jesus, who came to the lost sheep of the house of Israel, will gather into his fold "other sheep", and when by his redeeming work a people shall be born to the honour and glory of God. It will precede the time when God will be all and in all, the time spoken of in verse 10: "I will be thy king."

By a repetition of simple truths in different surroundings God has made it abundantly clear that promises made to Israel will be fulfilled, but the generation to whom they were spoken would perish in their sins. This principle is good for all time; God's kingdom will come, but many to whom the invitation has been given will not live to enjoy it. So the last chapter gathers together all the main teaching of the book into a tremendous exhortation to return unto the LORD our God; to observe the principles of God's salvation as they are seen in the teaching and experiences of Hosea.

14

"O ISRAEL, RETURN UNTO THE LORD THY GOD"
VERSES 1-3

O ISRAEL, return unto the LORD thy God; for thou hast fallen by thine iniquity.

2 Take with you words, and turn to the LORD: say unto him, Take away all iniquity, and receive us graciously: so will we render the calves of our lips.

3 Asshur shall not save us; we will not ride upon horses: neither will we say any more to the work of our hands, Ye are our gods: for in thee the fatherless findeth mercy.

TO appreciate fully the power of this closing exhortation it is necessary to see behind it the tragic story of Hosea's domestic life. We need to see the purchased Gomer, changed by her experiences; to hear her, now back at Hosea's side, appealing to Israel to return also. It is with an understanding of her folly and with the joy of her reinstatement that this chapter comes to life. Nor is the exhortation just for Israel, it is for the wise who "shall understand these things" and who will untimately declare "from me is thy fruit found" (v. 8).

Ever since the first transgression, man has been walking in the wrong direction and in the shadow cast by his own presence. The call comes to each to "return unto the LORD thy God". The two ways are divergent, so it is impossible to tread both at the same time. Jesus did not say "you must not serve God and mammon" but "you *cannot* serve God and mammon". We have seen demonstrated in Israel that sin very rarely arises from a direct

93

confrontation with God, but rather from the secret thought that it is possible to do one's own pleasure and still retain God's blessing. There is a vital need to face the facts and to return to God.

We have seen that man needs no help to destroy himself but that he does need help if he is to avoid destruction, so in this summary of his message Hosea makes this point again: "Thou hast fallen by thine iniquity." Israel had fallen and she had only herself to blame (cf. 7:8; 13:9). The nature we bear is prone to sin; we will find ourselves doing the things we would not, says Paul, and it is not without reason that sin is personified as a devil. In proving that there is no personal devil we must not destroy the reality of the power of sin. We must be ever conscious that apart from God's intervention we should all destroy ourselves, for we also "have fallen by our iniquity".

Again, confession is necessary: "Take with you words, and turn unto the LORD." It is true that He knows our need before ever we speak, but prayer is necessary; it crystallises our thoughts, it teaches humility, it expresses our dependence upon God and it increases our awareness of His presence. Notice the three stages:

1. Take away all iniquity;
2. Receive us graciously;
3. So will we render.

This is not just a confession of some besetting sin as though if only we could conquer it all would be well. This is a full and free confession that we are sinful people, that we have a corrupt nature and because of that we sin continually. It is a prayer that God will take away "all iniquity", that He will present us "faultless before the presence of his glory with exceeding joy". The prayer recognises that we have no rights before God and therefore it is by His grace alone that we can be made acceptable; but it also expresses a confidence that where there is a contrite heart He will receive us graciously. The final stage acknowledges that only in this way can we offer acceptable sacrifice to God: "So will we render the calves of our lips." With their lips they had kissed the idolatrous calves (13:2); now they would use their lips in true worship.

Such an expression of confidence in God must be accompanied by a complete denial of self and of any other source of strength. So here the people are led to confess the three alternative gods which they had taken to themselves, and to repent of their previous confidence in them:

1. "Asshur"—the Assyrians with whom they had made a covenant (12:1).
2. "Horses"—the horses and chariots of Egypt in which they had trusted (Isaiah 31:1).
3. "Idols"—the many strange gods they had made and served.

It is very evident from the examples stated that gods do not always assume the shape of idols, but are in the form of wealth, human wisdom, strength, or in fact anything upon which man may build his life. There is a very real difference between having riches and *trusting* in riches, as Jesus taught on many occasions. But we must always beware of the deceit in human nature which causes this fact to be used as an excuse to retain "the best" this world has to offer (cf. 1 Samuel 15:1-23).

The prayer concludes with a phrase which recognises that unlike the heathen gods, the LORD is a help of the helpless, for in Him "the fatherless find mercy". This understanding is fundamental to salvation since none is deserving of His mercy and no part of the Scriptures illustrates this better than the book we have been considering. We need only think of Hosea buying back Gomer, when she had nothing to commend her, and of that which is represented—Israel's complete unworthiness when God sought to help her—to understand how much we owe to God in that "whilst we were yet sinners, Christ died for us". James, whose epistle is full of practical exhortation, counsels that our understanding of this aspect of God's character must be reproduced in the lives of all who would be His servants. He writes, "Pure religion and undefiled before God and the Father is this, to visit the fatherless and widows in their affliction, and to keep himself unspotted from the world" (1:27).

"I WILL HEAL THEIR BACKSLIDING"

VERSES 4-9

4 *I will heal their backsliding, I will love them freely: for mine anger is turned away from him.*

5 *I will be as the dew unto Israel: he shall grow as the lily, and cast forth his roots as Lebanon.*

6 *His branches shall spread, and his beauty shall be as the olive tree, and his smell as Lebanon.*

7 *They that dwell under his shadow shall return; they shall revive as the corn, and grow as the vine: the scent thereof shall be as the wine of Lebanon.*

8 *Ephraim shall say, What have I to do any more with idols? I have heard him, and observed him: I am like a green fir tree. From me is thy fruit found.*

9 *Who is wise, and he shall understand these things? prudent, and he shall know them? for the ways of the LORD are right, and the just shall walk in them: but the transgressors shall fall therein.*

God's promised answer to this prayer is both immediate and full; as depicted in the parable of the prodigal son, God eagerly awaits signs of penitence that He might rush in to save! The Psalmist writes: "The LORD is nigh unto them that are of a broken heart; and saveth such as be of a contrite spirit" (34:18). He is near to all whose hearts are broken by His chastisement and is ready to move when contrition of spirit is expressed.

"I will heal their backsliding." This is much more than just the forgiveness of sins. It is healing the ravages of sin. It involves taking away transgressions and healing the nature which is the cause of such transgressions. As we see later in this chapter, it is part of the fulfilment of God's purpose.

"I will love them freely." How different this is from the grudging attitudes of man which often pass for forgiveness. Not only will God forgive and heal from the ravages of sin those who seek Him; He will also love them *freely*. Much has been written

96

about the love of God and how this seems to be crystallised in the use of the New Testament word *agape*, but nowhere is that love seen more clearly than in God's forgiveness. It permeates Old Testament history; it reaches a climax in the giving of His only begotten Son which is the life blood of the Gospel message. It is the basis of our hope, that we shall know that His "anger is turned away" from us.

The effect upon natural Israel of this healing is expressed under the figure of the revitalised land of Israel. The blooms of the lily, the firm root and foliage of the cedars, the fruitfulness of the olives, the corn and the vines: all enveloped in sweet fragrance. Psalm 133 describes a miraculous system of irrigation which God used as a source of blessing when the people were faithful and which will be used when His kingdom is established. It began with the rich dews which fell upon the mountain of Hermon in the north of the land and which were carried south by the gentle breezes to the hills of Zion. The Psalm shows how the blessing of the holy anointing oil ran from the beard of Aaron and thus over the Breastplate (Hermon) down the fringe of his garment and so on to the pomegranates (the seed of seeds). A picture is therefore given of the blessings which God has reserved for Israel which, having commenced with Christ, will also spread to cover the "sons of the living God", the New Jerusalem.

Contrast this dew of God with the dew of Israel: "Your goodness is as a morning cloud, and as the early dew it goeth away" (6:4) and "the early dew that passeth away" (13:3). Next notice the order of the blessings as stated in verses 5 and 6 and which in figure show the development of the true "sons of God". First the "lily" which is a symbol of purity; next the cedars representing strength and fruitfulness; then the beauty of the olives and the fragrance of Lebanon: purity, fruitfulness and fragrance. Man's order is to apply first a superficial fragrance and beauty, a mere veneer to cover what is within, whereas God commences with the heart. He first makes clean by "healing the backsliding" and then follows this with fruitfulness as He "loves them freely". Where there is purity and fruitfulness there will be natural beauty and fragrance. The effect

97

of this upon the new "sons of the living God" is that "they that dwell under his shadow shall return; they shall revive as the corn, and grow as the vine". In the new order which will be established, "the sons of the living God" will spread the blessings of God amongst the mortal population; they will teach all men concerning God and His ways. In that age God's people will say in all truth, "From me is thy fruit found".

Although the book of Hosea describes a true history of the ten tribe kingdom, the whole is also an acted parable to reveal God's work of salvation. It lays down clearly and with feeling, how the needs of man are met by our ever loving and merciful God but it also raises the question of our own participation. "Who is wise, and he shall understand these things? prudent, and he shall know them? for the ways of the LORD are right, and the just shall walk in them: but the transgressors shall fall therein."

CONCLUSIONS

IN the course of our study many devotional issues have been raised and whilst those most relevant to our theme have been treated fairly fully, others have been left for the reader to develop for himself. There are, however, some conclusions which may profitably be considered.

PARENTAL RESPONSIBILITIES

Hosea makes it abundantly clear that Israel had sinned and was herself responsible for her own destruction, but we can trace the root of this "degenerate plant of a strange vine" much further back into Israel's history.

The division of the Kingdom is said to be of God (1 Kings 12:24) but it must not be thought that God had planned this division from the beginning; rather that He had imposed the division as a punishment for the sinful behaviour of Solomon. "The cause was from the LORD, that he might perform his saying, which the LORD spake by Ahijah the Shilonite unto Jeroboam the son of Nebat" (1 Kings 12:15). To Solomon God had said, "Forasmuch as this is done of thee, and thou hast not kept my covenant and my statutes, which I have commanded thee, I will surely rend the kingdom from thee, and will give it to thy servant" (1 Kings 11:11).

David had spent his life building up and uniting the twelve tribes into the kingdom of power and splendour which was inherited by Solomon, but like so many sons who enter into their inheritance, Solomon did little further to consolidate the kingdom. Instead he squandered its wealth on great displays of majesty which resulted in the outrageous taxation of his subjects.

In Deuteronomy 17:14-18 we read of God's instructions which were to govern those elected to be king over His people. They include:

99

1. The king was to be of God's choosing.
2. He was not to be a stranger.
3. He was not to multiply horses. Instead he was to trust in God for his deliverance. .
4. He was not to return to Egypt.
5. He was not to multiply wives.
6. He was not to multiply silver and gold.
7. He was to copy for himself and read the law of God.

Each of these rules was completely disregarded by Solomon. His first act was to make an affinity with Pharaoh and take one of his daughters to be his wife (1 Kings 3:1). He multiplied horses and chariots (1 Kings 10:26), and silver and gold (v. 27). Not being satisfied with just multiplying wives, he took them from amongst the accursed peoples—Moabites, Ammonites, Edomites, Zidonians and Hittites (1 Kings 11:1). His disregard for the law of God was such that he built places of worship for the false gods of his wives in the hill which is before Jerusalem. All this resulted in his heir being born of an Ammonitish woman (1 Kings 14:31). The man whose name prefigured the King of Peace and who sat upon the throne in the City of Peace, was a man of discord and blatant wickedness who was responsible for the dividing of the kingdom of God. This division should never have taken place. As King Abijah said many years later to Jeroboam II: "Ought ye not to know that the LORD God of Israel gave the kingdom over Israel to David for ever, even to him and to his sons by a covenant of salt?" (2 Chronicles 13:5).

Strangely, the rebel king was "called out of Egypt" (1 Kings 12:2) just as many years later God would call His own Son out of Egypt. But unlike the true Son, Jeroboam was not to leave Egypt behind and his first act was to establish "strange gods". From that moment the ten tribe kingdom died (Hosea 13:1).

Although each is judged for his own sins, it must never be forgotten that the sins of parents can have far reaching effects amongst their children and children's children—for good or for evil!

Sometimes when parents recover from a lapse it is only to realise that the lapse had permanent and damaging effects upon their children. Happily it is sometimes seen that where parents subsequently forsake the Truth their children continue to follow their previous example. This principle must be recognised also in the family of the ecclesia: our responsibilities do not end with our own generation. We establish patterns of behaviour which, whether on a sound Scriptural basis or not, may continue to be accepted by those who follow.

"SHE IS NOT MY WIFE"

The real life parable of Hosea's broken marriage does provide some practical instruction which when added to other Bible teaching can be helpful towards a better understanding of present day problems. Because the subject is of such importance we will set out the stages along with the relevant quotations:

1. A marriage union should only be entered on the understanding that it will be for life (Genesis 2:24; Matthew 19:5; Romans 7:2; 1 Corinthians 7:10,11).

2. The above verses also teach that whilst marriage should be a life-long union, that union is not just a physical bond imposed at marriage, but a condition voluntarily accepted in response to God's command that we should make it so. Paul exhorts this in Ephesians 5 where he compares marriage to Jesus' relationship with the saints and where he uses similar language: "We are members of his body, of his flesh, and of his bones." In both cases the bond has to be sought in prayer. In marriage as in all aspects of discipleship it must involve body, mind and spiritual understanding.

3. Not only is there positive teaching that we should work at the "oneness" of marriage, there is direct counsel that we should not seek to destroy it: "Let not man put asunder"; "Let not the husband put away his wife"; "Let not the wife depart from her husband". To put away a partner incurs God's hatred (Malachi 2:16).

4. Hosea teaches the serious nature of the physical sins which defile marriage and sets out their consequences in unmistakable terms: "She is not my wife, neither am I her husband." This conclusion is also taught by other prophets: "Which my covenant they brake, although I was an husband unto them, saith the Lord" (Jeremiah 31:32); "And I will judge thee, as women that break wedlock and shed blood are judged" (Ezekiel 16:38). This is not a licence to break a marriage but a serious exhortation to avoid the kind of behaviour which does do so and for which one will then be answerable to God. The promiscuous behaviour of this age, which will become more prevalent as the days go by, must have no part in the lives of God's children. Before marriage the body must be preserved in purity to be presented as such to one's partner and during marriage our bodies are no longer our own to defile in illicit unions.

5. Perhaps the greatest lesson through Hosea is God's answer to the broken marriage. Under the Law a man who had given to his wife a Bill of Divorcement and whose wife had subsequently married again, was not permitted to take her back (Deuteronomy 24:1-4). It should be recognised that nowhere under the Law was divorce a legal requirement. All authorities will show that in Deuteronomy 24 the reading should be "*if* a man . . . " and so throughout the passage. This is shown to be the true meaning where this passage is quoted in Jeremiah 3:1, and is also the burden of Christ's confrontation with the Pharisees recorded in Matthew 19:3-9. The Pharisees' interpretation of the Mosaic Law was that it was a *commandment*; the question they had framed to test Jesus concerned the factors which would make the commandment operative. The Lord therefore first corrected their interpretation: "Moses because of the hardness of your hearts *suffered* you to put away your wives." Only then did he deal with any possible cause for divorce.

Once the "putting away" allowed by the Law had happened and re-marriage followed, what had been done could not be undone; the man's former wife was now "joined" to another. Perhaps this was behind the apostle Paul's teaching that those who have separated should remain unmarried or be reconciled again to their partner (1 Corinthians 7:11). A separation where chastity is maintained does not defile the marriage bond and leaves the way open for reconciliation. God reproved Judah for not observing this teaching (Jeremiah 3:1-3) but although Gomer had put herself in the impossible situation of being separated from Hosea and was instead "joined" to her lovers, Hosea does not leave her in her wickedness. At God's command he buys her back. In type Hosea shows that what man was not able to do for himself, God did for him through the death of His only begotten Son. The miracle of the salvation of men and women who by their lives have forsaken God and become "joined" to another is clearly taught by Hosea. There is no sin from which a man cannot be redeemed except blasphemy against the Holy Spirit.

Hosea does not tell us what he would have done had Gomer refused to go back with him. The story places before us the positive truth of the offer of salvation which God holds out to all who have sinned against Him. It does describe the dreadful alternative chosen by Israel, but it does not say what Hosea would have done had he been left by Gomer as God was by Israel. Only God could "buy back" as He did through His Son; man is powerless to act where there is an uncooperating partner. It is not part of the teaching of Hosea and such a digression would have obscured the main theme, but we are not left without guidance as can be seen in the writings of Paul (1 Corinthians 7).